ADOPTION REUNION

ECSTASY OR AGONY?

Evelyn Robinson

Clova Publications

Published by

Clova Publications
PO Box 328
Christies Beach
South Australia 5165
www.clovapublications.com

ISBN 978-0-9871931-2-4

First published in Australia in 2009
Reprinted in 2011

By the same author:

Adoption and Loss - *The Hidden Grief*

Adoption and Recovery – *Solving the mystery of reunion*

Adoption Separation - *Then and now*

~~~~~

CONTENTS

Introduction

A reunion between family members who have been separated by an adoption can be a very emotional event. For most people there is great joy and excitement, but for some there can be anger and disappointment. Sometimes there is a mixture of both ecstasy and agony. I have written this book to help to explain that mixture of feelings and to increase understanding of the emotional dynamics of the reunion experience. Although I live and work in South Australia, the information in this book is pertinent to anyone, anywhere in the world, who is interested in the outcomes of adoption separation and reunion.

Australia has led the English-speaking world in providing legal access to adoption information, which can facilitate reunion between adults separated by adoption. When children are adopted, they are no longer legally related to any member of their original families ie the family of their original mother and the family of their original father. When they become adults, however, many adopted people are reunited with their families of origin.

Formal, legal adoptions in South Australia commenced with the passing of the *Adoption Act 1925*. The peak period for adoptions in Australia was from the mid 1960s to the early 1970s. Numbers of adoptions of Australian-born children by people who were unknown and unrelated to the child prior to the adoption have reduced dramatically since that time. In 1971, there were almost one thousand such adoptions in South Australia; in 2008 there was only one. Although there are very few adoptions taking place nowadays in Australia, there are still many people who are experiencing the on-going impact of adoption in their lives.

In 1982 in Adelaide, South Australia, a conference was organised by the National Council for the Single Mother and her Child. Many mothers who had been separated from their children through adoption attended this conference and subsequently formed support organisations. As a result of pressure from these

4

and other adoption support groups, adults who had been adopted as children in Australia first gained a legal right to access their original birth certificates in the state of Victoria in 1984.

With the passing of the *Adoption Act 1988*, South Australia became the first state in Australia to grant equal rights to access identifying information to adults who had been adopted as children and to their original mothers. This means that when the adopted person reaches the age of eighteen, details of their adoptive identity can be made available to their original mother. At the same time, adults who were adopted as children may access their original birth certificate, which provides the identity of their original mother.

Conducting research into the long term outcomes of adoption separation and the impact of the reunion experience is a notoriously difficult undertaking, as it is impossible to guarantee a representative sample. I first became involved with post-adoption services in 1989 and, since then, I have been collecting material from many people who have experienced adoption separation and reunion and from professionals and volunteers working in post-adoption services.

In this book I have presented the conclusions I have reached after considering that material and reflecting on it. Those conclusions are informed by my personal experience of adoption separation and reunion and underpinned by my professional knowledge and experience as a counsellor and educator.

This book contains a selection from the many discussions I have had around adoption separation and reunion. Some of those discussions occurred twenty years ago and some in recent weeks. The responses which are recorded here have been condensed in order to provide a broad selection of topics and are, therefore, concise. When these issues were actually presented to me, they were, of course, addressed more fully and in greater depth.

Evelyn Robinson, 2009

This book is dedicated to my husband, Neil, who has enlivened my twilight years with his love, understanding and sense of adventure.

Adoption Loss and Grief

1. Grief of original mothers

Grief is the emotional reaction to a loss. There are losses other than death which give rise to grief reactions. One example is the loss experienced by the women (usually unmarried) who gave birth to children who were subsequently adopted (usually soon after birth) by someone else (usually a married couple, not related to the mother). The grief of the original mother of an adopted child is a unique experience and differs in fundamental ways from other grief experiences. Although the original fathers of adopted children often grieve also, as do some grandparents, siblings and other members of the extended families, their grief has its own qualities and is not the same as that of the mother who has physically carried her child and given birth.

There has been considerable discussion about whether or not useful research about the long term outcomes of adoption separation was available in the 1960s and 1970s, when so many adoptions took place in Australia, New Zealand, the United States, the United Kingdom, Canada and Ireland. My view is that it is impossible to assess accurately and usefully the outcomes of adoption separation, until some years after the event. Mothers often buried their grief throughout the years that their children were growing up. It was not until the child reached adulthood that the mother may have started to become aware of her loss and then her grief may have begun to surface. For adopted people, their grief may begin to stir in their teenage years, but it is often some years into adulthood before they are ready to consider reuniting with their original families. For many who have been separated by adoption, however, their grief is buried until much later in life.

For research to be useful, a significantly large sample group is required. For research on the long term outcomes of adoption separation to be useful in the 1960s, that sample group would need to have experienced adoption separation prior to the 1940s. At that time, not only were there few adoptions taking

9

place, but it was rare for those involved in adoptions to be willing to speak out about their experiences.

There were articles written in the 1960s and early 1970s, expressing opinions about the long term outcomes of adoption separation. However, it is unlikely that they were based on reliable research, either qualitative or quantitative, because a representative sample of the relevant population was not available.

Because there were so many adoptions in the 1960s and 1970s, however and because so many of those who were separated by adoption at that time have been willing to speak out, we do now have some data on which to form a view of the long term outcomes of adoption. This means that we now have the opportunity to plan confidently for the future, by learning from the experiences of the past. This long term perspective was not available forty years ago.

It was not until the numbers of adoptions started to reduce in the early 1970s that the relationship between original mothers and their adopted children began to be more generally acknowledged. It seems that the depth of the connection between the expectant mother and her unborn child had, before that time, been underestimated. The policy in many locations had been that children who were to be adopted should be removed from their mothers before a relationship between mother and child was able to develop. This attitude failed to recognise the fact that such a relationship may have already developed prior to the birth of the child. There was a belief that if mothers became emotionally attached to their children, this could interfere with the smooth flow of the adoption process and may have a detrimental impact on the child's ability to form attachments in the adoptive family.

As a result of this policy, many mothers whose children were subsequently adopted were prevented from seeing them and were sometimes deceived and told that their child had died, even though the original mother was still the child's legal parent prior

10

to the adoption order being granted and had every right to act as such without hindrance. Many original mothers report that they were unaware of their legal rights, however and felt disempowered throughout their experiences of pregnancy and childbirth.

Until recent years, similar steps were taken in cases of stillbirth and neo-natal death. Babies were often removed before the mothers were able to see them, mothers were often not allowed to name their children and no funeral was arranged. Nowadays, women who have lost children to stillbirth or neo-natal death are encouraged to hold their children, to have photographs taken, to keep mementoes such as locks of hair and handprints, to name their children and to talk about them.

Original mothers of adopted children lack a concrete focus for their grief. Many mothers were not allowed to see, hold or name their babies and they were not allowed to have a birth certificate as concrete evidence that they had had a child. In cases of stillbirth and neo-natal death, bonding is now actively encouraged, as it is believed that this facilitates the grieving process. In most cases of adoption, however, attempts were made after birth to prevent bonding. Attempts were also made in some hospitals to suppress grieving by the administration of drugs to mothers. More recently, mothers have been encouraged to spend time with their children before the separation occurs, but it will be some years before it will be clear whether or not this has made any significant difference to the grief that they suffer.

A further contributing factor was that the grief of the mother who had lost a child through adoption was generally not recognised by the community. These mothers were seldom visible in the community, because of the shame and secrecy involved in their experience of motherhood. The community perception was that, if a decision had been made for the child to be adopted, then this was because the mother had agreed for that to happen. Because mothers who had lost children through adoption generally did not talk about their loss, it appeared to others that they were not suffering. Mothers generally were told to 'get on with their lives' and because most of them appeared to be doing that, there was little recognition that they were suffering a degree of loss.

Because of the lack of recognition of their loss and the difficulties of finding a representative sample, there has been little incentive for academic research to be conducted into the outcomes of adoption separation for original mothers. However, I have found the information provided by the following authors to be supported by my experiences with the adoption community:

▶ *Shawyer (1979 & 1985)*

In 1979, Joss Shawyer, from New Zealand, wrote a book called *Death by Adoption*. In 1969, Shawyer was unmarried and pregnant with twins. She was appalled at the assumption that she would put her twins up for adoption and horrified at the pressure that was placed on her when she refused. Shawyer's book was groundbreaking, as it viewed adoption as a women's issue and explored the values underpinning adoption. Shawyer describes adoption as, '...a violent act, a political act of aggression towards a woman who has supposedly offended the sexual mores by committing the unforgivable act of not suppressing her sexuality' (Shawyer, 1979, p3). According to Shawyer the punishment for this unforgivable act is, 'She is stripped of her child by a variety of subtle and not so subtle manoeuvres and then brutally abandoned' (ibid p3).

Shawyer describes social workers who arranged adoptions as, 'Specially trained state-employed personnel...(who)...police her fall from grace and arrange to remove the product of her transgression to a safe and secret place' (Shawyer, 1979, p3). Shawyer describes how immature, unmarried mothers were persuaded to allow their children to be given to infertile, married women, supposedly 'for their own good'. Shawyer also tells the stories of adopted people. Her book also includes an interview with an adoptive mother and an interview with an involuntarily childless woman who did not adopt.

Joss Shawyer also published an article in the magazine *Healthright*, called *The Politics of Adoption* (Shawyer, 1985). In it she states, 'I have never heard of a case where adoption had a good effect upon the original mother, but until women who have lost children this way speak out publicly about their suffering, society will go on unchallenged, justifying this inhumane practice' (Shawyer, 1985, p27). Shawyer's explanation for why the suffering of the original mother has been kept hidden for so long is that, '...once her consent (and with it the baby) has been obtained she herself is of no further consequence' (ibid p27). There appears to have been a perception among professionals that there was no need for counselling to be provided for mothers after their children had been removed from them.

▶ *Silverman (1981)*
Phyllis Silverman is the author of a book entitled *Helping Women Cope with Grief* (1981). This is one of a few books that tackle the issue of the grief of original mothers of adopted children directly. In the introduction to her book, Silverman points out that she is addressing the issues of women who have found themselves in situations, '...for which their previous experience has not prepared them' (Silverman, 1981, p9). Her book is directed at those in the helping professions. Silverman describes how so many original mothers suppressed their grief and how this suppressed grief manifested itself, in feelings of guilt, anger, tenseness and fear of discovery (ibid p60). Silverman goes on to say that, '...the pain, secrecy and guilt involved in their experience can profoundly affect their future marriages' (ibid p61). Silverman also points out that some original mothers of adopted children later marry in order to gain approval from parents, who, '...had expressed disappointment or disgust with their previous pregnancies' (ibid

p61). Silverman describes the impact of revealing the secret (of having had a child who was adopted) as a 'thawing out', as original mothers sometimes describe themselves after disclosing their status, '...as having been in a deep freeze, sometimes for years' (ibid p66). Silverman acknowledges the importance of support groups for original mothers and says that without such an understanding and sympathetic forum, many mothers would remain in hiding, postponing or even indefinitely deferring their accommodation to their grief (ibid p69).

► *Winkler, van Keppel, Midford, Cicchini (1982, 1984 & 1987)*
Robin Winkler and Margaret van Keppel presented a paper at the Third Australian Adoption Conference in 1982. In this paper they compared the loss of a child through adoption with other losses and pointed out its two main distinguishing features (Winkler & van Keppel, 1982, p175). The first is that the original mother may feel responsible for the decision to give up the child for adoption and therefore may consider the loss as a self-inflicted one. This can result in feelings of guilt, shame and powerlessness. The second is that the child is lost to the mother, but still lives and so there is always the possibility of a reunion. This means that there is a lack of finality to the loss. These are the two most important factors, in their opinion, which make resolution of the original mother's grief exceptionally difficult.

In 1984, Winkler and van Keppel conducted a study of two hundred and thirteen women, Australia-wide, who had lost a first child through adoption (Winkler & van Keppel, 1984). They found that the effects of the loss of the child on the mother were both negative and long lasting. All of the mothers who participated in the study reported a sense of loss, which did not diminish over time. In fact, approximately half of the mothers surveyed reported an increase in the sense of loss over time. The mothers involved in the Winkler and van Keppel study were volunteers, most of whom responded to requests in the media.

At a conference in 1987, Margaret van Keppel, Suzanne Midford and Mercurio Cicchini presented a paper in which they pointed out that there were often additional stressful life-events connected with the loss of a child through adoption (van Keppel, Midford & Cicchini, 1987, p44). Many original mothers had to move to another residence or sometimes to another town during their pregnancy in order to avoid the shame and embarrassment for themselves and their families. For many, the pregnancy meant the end of their relationship with the father of their child. Some were forced by the pregnancy to leave study or employment. The pregnancy caused an irreversible change in the relationship between the original mother and her parents, whether the parents were aware of the pregnancy or not. The pregnancy often drove a wedge between the expectant mother and her friends. Original mothers often resented their friends for their freedom and their hopes for the future.

As a result of these changes, many original mothers felt very isolated at the time of their pregnancies. Most original mothers were immature and unable to cope with this combination of stressful events all occurring at the same time. After enduring the pregnancy, often in social isolation, they were then required to make a decision regarding their child's future. Van Keppel, Midford and Cicchini noted that it was not uncommon for mothers who had lost children to adoption to experience difficulties in forming or maintaining significant relationships and they relate this to the fact that the relinquishment of the child was coupled with other traumatic events (van Keppel, Midford & Cicchini, 1987, p45).

▶ *Inglis (1984)*
In 1984, Kate Inglis wrote a book called *Living Mistakes*, which is sub-titled, *Women who consented to adoption* (Inglis, 1984). Her book grew out of her observation that women who were recounting their reproductive histories and revealed that they had

lost a child through adoption, '...exhibited a pattern of behaviour in the telling which centred on an unresolved grief and an ambivalence about their motherhood' (Inglis, 1984, p18). Inglis goes on to say that, 'Their isolation in both the event and the memory was striking'. Inglis states that while anger is a common response to loss and a recognised component of grief, 'Anger is also a likely consequence following relinquishment' (ibid p170). She goes on to describe many of the ways in which original mothers of adopted children are angry and many of the ways in which that anger can be expressed. She also acknowledges that in many cases it remains unexpressed. Inglis says of the original mother, 'She may begin her pregnancy in anger and resentment and continue for years with a randomly placed rage' (ibid p170).

▶ *Condon (1986)*

Dr John Condon of Flinders Medical Centre, South Australia, conducted some research in 1986. In his South Australian study of twenty original mothers, he found, '...a very high incidence of pathological grief reactions which have failed to resolve although many years have elapsed since the relinquishment' (Condon, 1986, p117). Condon also recorded that more than half of the women he surveyed reported that their anger had increased since the time of relinquishment (ibid p118).

Long term outcomes

The research which is available indicates that original mothers of adopted children may carry their grief with them for many years and that it does not evaporate over time. Results highlight their anger and sense of loss and the fact that these can often increase with the passage of time. This research, of course, has been conducted among English-speaking mothers. In recent years many children have been removed from their families in developing countries and adopted into affluent countries. It may be many years before the issues for those mothers receive similar attention.

16

2. *Grief of adopted people*

The feelings of loss experienced by adults who were adopted as children have not always been apparent and so too often the assumption has been that those feelings did not exist. As their original mothers appeared to 'get on with their lives' and often showed no outward signs of their inner turmoil, so adopted children often appeared to be content with their lot and showed no obvious signs of grieving.

It is now generally accepted that adopted people can experience a deep and painful sense of loss because they have been separated from their original mothers and families. Their grief resulting from this loss is not always obvious and is often exhibited indirectly in the behaviour of adopted people, especially in the adolescent years.

For some adopted people, the fact that they were not raised in their original families causes them to feel rejected and abandoned. They suffer from the loss of their relationship with their original parents, the loss of kinship by being separated from their extended families and community and the loss of identity from not knowing exactly who they are.

Because adopted people usually have no conscious memory of the separation from their original families, they also lack a concrete focus for their grief. There is no finality to their grief, as they know that they have other families somewhere and that they will always, in some way, be a part of those families. Even if they are told that they are adopted, many questions and mysteries remain.

It could be that the work produced in the 1970s and 1980s addressing the issues for original mothers encouraged further exploration in the 1980s and 1990s of the issues for adults who were adopted as children. I have found the information provided by the following authors to be supported by my experiences with the adoption community:

17

▶ *Small (1987)*

Joanne Small is an adopted person and a clinical social worker. She is the author of an article entitled, *Working with Adoptive Families*, which was published in a journal called *Public Welfare* in 1987. The article is sub-titled, *We must come to see that families who adopt are not the same as others*. Small describes how adoptive families operate to deny the difference between raising adopted children and raising one's own natural children. A result of this denial, according to Small, is that, '...the child's basic sense of self develops around a faulty belief system' (Small, 1987, p36). This is obviously damaging to the developing child who is trying to establish his or her identity and place in the family and in the world. Small describes some of the characteristics which she observed in adoptive families; for example, family members have difficulty identifying and expressing their feelings about adoption, there is a tendency toward perfectionism and unrealistic expectations, fantasy replaces reality, there are feelings of powerlessness, members of the family feel responsible for the feelings of others, members of the family share low self esteem and family members show a strong need for approval (ibid p36).

Small also describes the denial which exists among professionals who work with adopted people of the importance in their lives of having been adopted. Small says, 'We must recognize the role of denial among professionals working with adoptive families, some of whom are themselves members of adoptive families and many of whom are unwittingly engaged in codependent roles' (Small, 1987, p41). Small calls for training to be provided to professionals, which should include, '...an understanding of the differences in adoptive family structure, the role of denial in adoptive families, the meaning and effects of codependence on professionals and adoptive family members' among other factors (ibid p41). Small describes the denial practised by adopted people. She says, 'Adult children of adoption also carry with them a strong tendency to deny that adoption can be the basis for their problems' (ibid p40). Small goes on to describe how adopted people can let go of this denial by searching for their original parents. Small says that, 'Adult children who search have chosen to give up the denial' (ibid p40). Small recommends that adopted people attend support groups in order to share their experiences and gain strength from the support of others who have also been adopted. In this way their innermost feelings can be validated rather than denied.

► *Verrier (1991 & 1993)*

Nancy Verrier is an adoptive mother and a clinical psychologist. She presented a paper at the American Adoption Congress International Convention in 1991 and later expanded it into a book called *The Primal Wound* (Verrier, 1993). Verrier spoke at the convention of the 'staggering' statistics which show that although adopted people make up 2-3% of the population in the United States, they make up 30-40% of the young people in 'special schools, juvenile hall [detention centres] and residential treatment centres' (Verrier, 1991). In this paper, Verrier described how the adopted person's perception of having been abandoned by their original mother can affect their feelings of self-worth in a negative way and cause them to have a constant fear of further abandonment. Verrier explained that this fear of abandonment can result in hyper-vigilance on the part of the child, which is why so many adopted people suffer from free-floating anxiety and psychosomatic illnesses, especially unexplained stomach-aches, headaches and allergies.

Verrier spoke of the separation of the child from the original mother as an experience 'from which neither fully recovers' and said that the adopted person, in losing the sense of well being and security of the presence of their original mother, had 'lost something which could never be regained'. Verrier also spoke about the phenomenon of adopted people sabotaging their birthdays, because the anniversary for them represents sorrow and parting, not joy. In this paper, Verrier also explained that adopted people often apparently make a 'good adjustment' to their adoption, but what this means is simply that they learn how to seek approval and to suppress their true feelings.

Verrier wrote in 1993 of the pain experienced by adopted people and of the difficulties of finding professionals who are aware of the issues for adoptive families. In *The Primal Wound* (1993), Verrier describes how many adoptive parents believe that all their adopted children need is to be loved and how, as adopted children grow up, parents often have difficulty understanding their testing-out behaviour. Verrier also explains that she finally came to understand that it is sometimes difficult for adopted children to accept the love that their adoptive parents want to give them and that this testing-out behaviour is, '...one of two diametrically opposed responses to being abandoned, the other being a tendency toward acquiescence, compliance and withdrawal' (Verrier, 1993, Preface). Verrier says that it sometimes takes years of therapy for adopted people to get in touch with their feelings of rejection. Verrier found that adopted people were, 'greatly over-represented in psychotherapy', that they '...demonstrated a high incidence of juvenile delinquency, sexual promiscuity and running away from home' and that they consistently showed symptoms which were 'impulsive, provocative, aggressive and antisocial' (ibid).

Verrier writes about the difference between attachment and bonding. She says that adopted children form an attachment to their adoptive parents because they quickly come to realise that their survival depends on it, but that they may never truly bond with them (Verrier, 1993, p19). Verrier points out that bonding begins in the womb and is exhibited by the fact that, in the crucial period immediately following birth, new-born babies have been shown to recognise their mothers, through smell, heartbeat, voice and eye contact. The child is born with the expectation that its life will revolve around the person with whom it has become familiar for nine months. When this does not happen, when this continuum is broken by the child suddenly being handled by a different person ie the adoptive mother, the baby can be left feeling, '...hopeless, helpless, empty, and alone' (ibid p21). Verrier goes on to state that, '...the severing of that connection...causes a primal or narcissistic wound...which manifests in a sense of loss, basic mistrust, anxiety and depression, emotional and/or behavioural problems, and difficulties in relationships with significant others' (ibid p21).

▶ *Lifton (1994)*

Betty Jean Lifton is an adopted person, a counselling psychologist and the author of several books on adoption topics. In 1994, Lifton wrote *Journey of the Adopted Self*, in which she explores the impact of adoption on adopted people. Lifton describes the two opposing responses of adopted people, which are particularly noticeable during adolescence, when she describes the compliant adopted people who, because of their issues of unresolved grief and loss, '...pay the price with eating disorders, phobias, and an underlying depression' while others, '...take an oppositional stance to anyone who tries to control them, be they parents, school teachers, or legal authorities' (Lifton, 1994, p66). In many families where there are two adopted children, it is common for one child to be compliant and the other to be rebellious. This was described to me by one adoptive mother as, *One shuts up and the other acts up.*

Lifton goes on to say that adopted children, '...often do not feel entitled to express any negative feelings, such as grief or anger at being cut off from their origins' (Lifton, 1994, p30) and points out that this anger often displays as depression (ibid p89). It also, however, often 'manifests itself in destructive, acting-out behaviour' (ibid p91). Lifton gives as a possible cause of the over-representation of adopted people in psychiatric wards, '...the difficulty many young adoptees have repressing their grief and anger and sense of powerlessness' (ibid p91) and says, 'Therapists should not be asking why adopted children are angry, but why shouldn't they be?' (ibid p89). Lifton also points out that many adoptive parents find these ideas threatening. She says, 'The need to idealize the institution of adoption in order to ward off their own fears unfortunately prevents these parents from being in touch with their children's pain' (ibid p91).

Lifton also writes about the trauma associated with adoption and the '...high psychic cost that both parent and child pay when they repress their grief and loss' (Lifton, 1994, p8). She goes on to say that, in her opinion, '...it is unnatural for members of the human species to grow up separated from...their natural clan' and that because of the effects of this separation on adopted people, 'They grow up feeling like anonymous people cut off from the genetic and social heritage that gives everyone else roots' (ibid p8). Lifton is aware that this news is not often well received by adoptive parents. She cautions them that if they love their children they will have empathy for the sorrow that they experience not, '...turn on the professionals who describe it' (ibid p33). Lifton writes about adopted people being 'strong enough' to claim their heritage (ibid p47), when they search for their original parents and describes how in children who have been adopted, lack of knowledge about their origins 'interferes with the child's struggle to form an early sense of self' and that '...not even the most loving adoptive parents...can soften the psychic toll that...exacts from the child' (ibid p49). Lifton describes how an Artificial Self is created. She describes the Artificial Self as being '...compliant, afraid to express its real feelings, such as sadness or anger, for fear of losing the only family it has' (ibid p52).

Lifton describes separation anxiety and how it exists in adoptive families. She states that many adopted people have difficulty separating from their adoptive parents, even to attend school. The reason these difficulties arise is that any separation resurrects the feelings of loss related to the original separation from the mother. Lifton also says that some adopted people

22

deliberately choose to become indispensable to their adoptive parents to ensure that they will not be abandoned by them and therefore not have to undergo yet another separation (Lifton, 1994, p70). According to Lifton, children were often adopted to fulfil the desires and fantasies of their adoptive parents. Many adopted people, even into adulthood, feel an unhealthy responsibility for ensuring that their adoptive parents are happy. Some never outgrow the compliant attitude they practised as they were growing up. For other adoptees, the search for an identity leads them to choose a negative identity in order to associate with the impression they have obtained from their adoptive parents that their original parents were somehow defective (ibid p71).

Lifton mentions the fact that sexual promiscuity is common among adopted people. She says, 'Both male and female adoptees give themselves freely to others out of a sense of worthlessness or as a way of trying to get close to another person. Physical intimacy gives them the illusion of love' (Lifton, 1994, p72). Lifton also refers to David Kirschner, who, she says, found that adopted people often exhibited, '...deceptive charm that covered over a shallowness of attachment' (ibid p92).

▶ *Pavao (1997)*

Adoption losses are particularly obvious in the cases of cross-cultural adoptions. This was very poignantly illustrated by Dr Joyce Maguire Pavao at the Adoption and Healing Conference in New Zealand in 1997. Dr Pavao is an adopted person and a family therapist. She told the story of a young man called Trevor who attempted suicide when he was thirteen years old. Trevor had been adopted from Colombia when he was four years old by an American family, described by Pavao as, '...very affluent, a white family who lived in a beautiful suburb of Boston'. Dr Pavao tried to help the young man find a reason to go on living. His response to her was, 'You don't understand, Joyce, I can't live. I'm dead. I have been dead since I was four or five years old. My name was

23

Ricardo. I spoke Spanish. I lived in another country, I was another person and I have been trying very hard to be this new person and I can't do it, I just can't do it.' (Pavao, 1997, p200).

Long term outcomes

Research undertaken among adopted people shows that many of them grieve for the loss of their original mothers and families and that this grief can affect their feelings of self-worth and their ability to form close relationships with other people.

Because the stigma associated with out-of-wedlock births has reduced dramatically in Australia, as in other English-speaking countries and because financial assistance is more readily available to unmarried mothers, very few children are now being separated from their mothers to be adopted. As the numbers of Australian-born children being adopted has reduced, the numbers of children born in other countries and adopted into Australia has increased. While mothers in Australia are being supported to raise their children, this is not always the case for mothers in other countries.

The issues of loss and grief are intensified for those who are adopted into a different racial and/or cultural background from the one into which they were born, especially when they are removed from their country of origin. We are beginning to hear now from those adults who were adopted interracially and our societies are beginning to acknowledge the additional losses experienced in those situations.

In February 2008 the Prime Minister of Australia formally apologised to Indigenous Australians for the fact that so many of them were separated from their families of origin and raised apart from them. There have been calls for a similar apology to non-Indigenous Australians who were removed from their families to be adopted and also to those who were removed from their countries of birth and adopted into Australia.

3. Disenfranchised grief

Mourning

I have used my experiences in the adoption field for the last twenty years to formulate an explanation for the grief which I have found to be present in adoption separation experiences and especially evident at the time of reunion. Two authors who have studied grief and loss extensively are William Worden (an American professor and author of *Grief Counselling and Grief Therapy*, 1991) and Beverley Raphael (an Australian professor and author of *The Anatomy of Bereavement*, 1983*)*.

According to Worden, grief is the personal experience of loss, while mourning is the process through which people pass (Worden, 1991). Worden describes four phases of mourning and four tasks of mourning. These phases and tasks serve a useful purpose for those who have experienced a loss. They are the process by which grievers are able to come to terms with their loss and move forward. It is important to be aware that the aim of mourning is not to lead the bereaved back to the position which they occupied before their loss occurred. Worden is very clear that trying to achieve this would suggest a failure to perform the tasks of mourning (Worden, 1991, p18). The purpose of grieving is to lead the mourners forward so that they can incorporate the grief into their lives and learn to find a place for it.

The first phase of mourning, as outlined by Worden, is usually *numbness*, when people have difficulty accepting what has happened. The second is *yearning*, when people become angry and want the event to be undone. The third phase is *disorganisation and despair*, when mourners find it difficult to function and the fourth is what Worden calls *reorganised behaviour* when the mourner is beginning to regain equilibrium. The tasks of mourning described by Worden are firstly, to accept the reality of the loss, secondly, to work through the pain of grief, thirdly, to adjust to an environment in which the deceased is

25

missing and fourthly, to relocate the deceased emotionally and move on with life. Ideally, when these phases and tasks have been completed, the loss will be more manageable.

What is disenfranchised grief?

In his book *Disenfranchised Grief*, Kenneth Doka describes some situations in which it is not possible for grievers to pass through the phases and tasks of mourning, because their grief is 'disenfranchised' ie not recognised and supported by the community. Other authors such as David Meagher, Jeffrey Kauffman, Vanderlyn Pine, Jane Nichols and Dale Kuhn also contributed to the book. Doka describes disenfranchised grief as grief connected to a loss which cannot be openly acknowledged, publicly mourned or socially supported (Doka, 1989, p4). He expands on this description by saying that in many cases of disenfranchised grief, either the relationship is not recognised, the loss is not recognised or the griever is not recognised (ibid pp5-6).

Doka points out that, 'Most of the losses we experience are not due to physical death' (Doka, 1989, p116). Doka describes feelings of bereaved persons such as anger, guilt, sadness, depression, hopelessness and numbness (ibid p70) and states that these reactions can be complicated when grief is disenfranchised. The mourners whose grief is disenfranchised are, by virtue of this, cut off from social supports and so have few opportunities to express and resolve their feelings.

Doka also states that, '...significant losses can occur even when the object of the loss remains physically alive' (Doka, 1989, p6) and he acknowledges that, '...we are just becoming aware of the sense of loss that people experience in giving children up for adoption' (ibid).

Disenfranchised grief and shame

The grief of those who have experienced adoption separation has been disenfranchised for several reasons and in several ways.

Because the pregnancy and birth of the child were often kept totally secret because of the shame involved, many original mothers of adopted children had no choice but to conceal their grief also. This meant that their loss was seldom openly acknowledged. In many cases, original mothers were told by family members, by friends, by medical staff or by religious personnel, that they were 'doing the right thing'. This, in fact, constitutes a denial of the legitimacy of their grief and so they often felt guilty and ashamed and thought that their grief was caused by selfishness or self-pity. This meant that their loss was seldom socially supported. The result of this denial of their feelings was often a deepening of those feelings. Many original mothers will agree with Meagher that, '...denial does not cause feelings to disappear, in fact they grow in intensity' (Meagher, 1989, p320). Kauffman states that, '...the specific psychological phenomenon operating in disenfranchised grief is shame' (Kauffman, 1989, p25). Because of their shame, their loss was seldom publicly mourned.

Shame is a word used by many original mothers to describe their feelings at the time of their pregnancy. Some women were so ashamed that they did not even tell their parents that they were pregnant. Numbers of adoptions in South Australia gradually increased from the introduction of the *Adoption Act* in 1925 until 1972, when numbers of adoptions began to reduce. During this period, being unmarried and pregnant was considered to be a shameful condition. In some countries this is still the case and women, rather than men, are usually the objects of blame and punishment.

Adoption was seen, during that period, as the solution to what society viewed as a problem. Through adoption it was thought that the unmarried mother would be rescued from her shameful state and the child would be rescued from the stigma of illegitimacy. Many original mothers found, however, that far from feeling rescued, they ultimately felt ashamed, either of having

27

been unable to resist being pressured into agreeing to the adoption or of having been unable to prevent the adoption taking place. It is no wonder that many original mothers found it impossible to confront their grief, as their shame led them to believe that their grief was not legitimate.

Kauffman states that shame can lead to a fear of abandonment (Kauffman, 1989, p26). Many original mothers describe how for them the risk of abandonment was too great to allow them to share their grief with anyone. Because of their fears their sadness grew secretly within them and they spent many years hiding the fact that they had lost a child through adoption. They feared that they would lose the approval of friends and family members if their secret became known and so they suffered in silence. For many, this has inhibited the resolution of their grief.

When adopted people grow up in a family where the adoption is not acknowledged, they may sense a feeling of shame attached to adoption. This can be more intense if the adoption is concealed from the adopted person until they reach adulthood.

Disenfranchised grief and silence
One of the simplest, yet most therapeutic ways of dealing with a loss is to talk about it to a sympathetic listener. Kuhn discusses the role of silence in the blocking of grief resolution and states that this often occurs, '...when a loss is unusual, or a person who has been lost...(is)...unknown to the family' (Kuhn, 1989, p241). He states that some people, '...feel awkward about expressing their feelings for fear that others will not understand' (ibid p241) and that this reluctance to express grief can lead to the person suffering in silence. This has been the experience of many mothers who lost children through adoption.

Kuhn expands on the issue of silence by saying that it has its roots in, '...the defenses of denial, repression, or suppression' (Kuhn, 1989, p244). Because mourners do not feel it is safe to express their grief, '...a cycle of silence...gets established' (ibid p244). Kuhn goes on to describe how a communal silence develops which often happens because the community blames the mourner for having made a bad choice. The communal silence is often interpreted by the mourner as disapproval and this reinforces the sense of shame already felt by the mourner. This means that the loss is not dealt with, which can lead to 'depression and other mental disorders' (ibid p245). Kuhn stresses the importance of breaking the silence in order to begin to address, '...the chaos that loss often brings – especially loss that seems atypical and is connected with guilt' (ibid p247).

Meagher also refers to the silence factor. He states that grief is often complicated when there is a need for concealment. The reason that the grief of the original mother is concealed is that, 'Revelation may result in a more intense negative social response' (Meagher, 1989, p315). As a result of this concealment many original mothers develop an anger and resentment against what they perceive to be society's abandonment of them. Shawyer puts this very succinctly when she says, 'Of course everybody knows that if she really loves the child, she will give it away and too late she discovers what 'everybody' knew all along but conveniently forgot to share with her – the knowledge that if she had really loved the child she would never have given it up!' (Shawyer, 1979, p5). Many original mothers feel betrayed by a society which told them to be unselfish and sign adoption consents because it would be best for their children and then made them feel ashamed of their actions afterwards.

Silence has also been a factor affecting the grief of adopted people. Many adoptive parents have been open with their children about their adoptive status and for them it has never been a secret. However, in some families, the adoption was announced once and then never discussed again. Adopted children may assume from the behaviour of others that adoption is something not very pleasant, a topic not to be discussed but to be avoided. When adoptive parents do not correct visitors who, unaware of the

29

nature of family relationships, claim to see a genetic resemblance between parents and children, for example, the adopted child may form the impression that adoption is something unmentionable and that other people are better left in the dark.

Disenfranchised grief and ritual
Anthropologists have discovered a wide variety of funeral rites throughout the ages and throughout the world and it is clear that almost every society has created a series of activities to assist the bereaved to adjust to their loss. Rituals provide the bereaved with permission to mourn. Pine discusses Freud's notion that grieving allows the griever to obtain, '...a kind of 'freedom' from the dead person' (Pine, 1989, p14). Many original mothers feel that because they were not permitted to grieve, they have not been able to achieve that 'freedom' and so their mourning remains unresolved. The families and friends of original mothers are often surprised many years later to hear of the pain that they have suffered because their grief at the time was 'apparently absent'. Pine points out that this apparent absence of grief can, in fact, be a sign of acute grief which has been repressed and/or delayed (ibid p15).

Pine states that the purposes of funeral rites include; announcing the death, recognising the place which the dead person held in society, assisting the bereaved through the process of grief, delimiting the period of mourning, allowing the grievers to express their emotions publicly and allowing the members of the community to gather to support each other (Pine, 1989, p13). Pine comments on the 'pathological reactions to bereavement' caused by 'the absence of understood social expectations and acceptable rituals for mourning' (ibid p17). Often at the funeral, or the wake, friends and family members recall events in the life of the deceased person and discuss his or her personal characteristics. This provides comfort and reassurance to the bereaved. The recollection of happy events can bring a positive note to a sad occasion.

For the original mother of an adopted child, there was generally no formal announcement of the birth or the adoption of her child; in fact the activity often took place in secret. Her child was not given the opportunity to be granted a place in society as the procedure of adoption denied the child's place in the original family. Frequently no one assisted the original mother through the process of grief, as there was usually no recognition that she had suffered a loss (because she apparently 'agreed' to the adoption). Because there was no ritual to delimit the period of mourning, many original mothers describe their grief as 'a life sentence'. Original mothers seldom had the opportunity to express their grief publicly at the time of their loss, as society was embarrassed by their situation and did not grant them acceptance or permission to grieve. There was no gathering of the community around the original mother. Instead she was often shunned and ostracised by her community. There were no happy recollections to comfort her.

At the time of the birth and adoption, there were no rituals to assist original mothers to accept the loss of their children. They were not given any document to prove that they had, in fact, given birth. One of the recommendations of the Third Australian Conference on Adoption held in Adelaide in 1982 was that original parents be provided with documentation relating to the adoption as well as access to original birth certificates at all times.

In most countries, adopted people are not given copies of their original birth certificates until they become adults and may then apply for them. In some places, adopted people can never access their original birth certificates. Many adopted people are not even aware that they have two birth certificates. Some adopted people, as a way of reclaiming their identity, change their names back to the original, once they have their original birth certificates. Many adopted people feel that because they were infants at the time of the adoption, it was something that was done without their knowledge or consent and therefore experience feelings of anger and powerlessness. There are no accepted rituals for them, as adults, to help them to come to terms with their adoption loss. The lack of ritual is another factor that prevents the grief of the original mother and the adopted person from being resolved.

Outcomes of disenfranchised grief
Grief is repressed or delayed when there are no opportunities to move through the phases and tasks of mourning. Whereas traditionally mourners would turn to their families for emotional support, because in many cases original mothers were perceived as having brought shame on the family, that avenue of support was often closed to them. Many original mothers report that after the loss of their child, friends and family members either avoided their company or when in their company, avoided any mention of the pregnancy or the lost child. In this way it often appeared to the original mother that those around her were colluding with society to deny her experience and her loss. In fact those people, like the original mother herself, had no previous experience that was comparable to this one on which to draw and were probably at a loss as to how to react. The practice in some countries of issuing the adopted child with a new birth certificate, which states that the adoptive mother gave birth to the child, allows public denial of the existence of the original mother and therefore of her loss.

Kauffman states that when grief is disenfranchised, '...the bereaved may become disillusioned with and alienated from their community' (Kauffman, 1989, p29) and that this can affect one's sense of identity and belonging. Many original mothers and adopted people speak of feeling isolated and misunderstood by society in general.

Because family members separated by adoption are not supported to work through the phases and tasks of mourning, owing to the impact of shame, silence and the lack of ritual around their loss, their grief is often buried and remains unacknowledged.

32

4. Questions asked by original parents

I've thought of searching for the son I gave up for adoption but some people are telling me that it would be selfish of me to contact him. I don't want to ruin his life by intruding. Do I have the right to do that?

Everyone who knows they have been adopted knows that they have an original mother and an original father. They also know, therefore, that there is a possibility of a reunion with their original parents. Some have anticipated those events and have chosen to prepare themselves and others have chosen not to prepare themselves. You have no way of knowing how ready your son might be to meet you again, but you can let him know that you care about him and allow him to make an informed decision about the opportunity you are offering him. I don't think that making contact with your son would be selfish. In fact, I believe that it is a very generous act.

Some people say that adopted people who search for their original parents mostly just do it out of curiosity and that they usually only want information, not a relationship. Do you think that's true?

I believe that one of the principal reasons that family members who have been separated by adoption seek each other is to be able to work through their grief. They are generally not consciously aware of this, of course, at the time of making the decision to search. Many people say after they have been reunited that they didn't understand why they had searched until after the reunion had taken place. Adopted people often say that they search out of curiosity and that's true. At a very basic level, that's what it is. On a deeper level, however, I believe that they are seeking a more complete sense of self, which can be achieved by addressing the impact of adoption on their lives. They are often afraid to say that they would like to have an on-going relationship, as they don't want to be disappointed if it doesn't

33

eventuate. In my view it is a quite understandable aspect of human nature to want to seek out those to whom we are related. So many people research their family histories because they feel that knowledge of their ancestors contributes to their self-knowledge. People also seek out family members from whom they have been separated, even when no adoption has taken place. As adults, we choose which family connections we wish to nurture and maintain.

It's wonderful to have my daughter back in my life, but sometimes I feel that I'm the one making all the effort in the relationship. I get tired of it. Why doesn't she make an effort to show me that she's interested?

You have to remember that, although you are both adults, you are the parent in this relationship. You have a conscious memory of the closeness which you and your daughter once shared, while she does not. You have had the opportunity of more years to experience life, to mature and to prepare for this reunion. As the parent, you will always have those advantages. Parents are generally expected to set an example for their children. Adopted people sometimes find it difficult to accommodate their complex family ties. Just remember that she doesn't owe you anything and that any contact you have with her is a bonus. I have never understood why some people seem to think it's useful in relationships to keep a mental record of who initiates each contact. I don't see that there's anything to be gained by keeping score. I would suggest that you try to be glad that you know her and enjoy the time you have with her.

I was reunited with my daughter some years ago and her life is a real mess. She's very demanding and her constant crises are affecting my life, my health and the other members of my family. I just feel that I can't cope with this any more. I've been told not to walk away from her, as she will feel as if she's been abandoned twice. What should I do?

It's very difficult to be reunited with a family member and to find that their values and their way of life are very different from your own. It is often easier for parents to be tolerant towards the children that they have raised, because they knew them and can remember them when they were innocent and vulnerable. With a child one did not raise, it is often more difficult to set boundaries. Some original parents feel that somehow they have to try to make up for the fact that they allowed their children to be adopted and they fear that if they withdraw support from their adult child, then that child will disappear out of their life again. Only you can decide firstly, at what point you have given so much and can give no more and secondly, to what extent you are helping your child or perhaps instead supporting her in a lifestyle that is not conducive to her own well-being. It's also about creating some kind of balance among all of the relationships which exist in your life and finding a place for this one where it will sit comfortably and not overshadow the others. In the initial phases of reunion, this is often what happens, but after some time there is usually a reduction in the original intensity. This allows those involved to have more emotional energy to devote to the other important people in their lives. When this happens you will not be abandoning her any more than you did when she was adopted.

I've been reunited with the son that I lost to adoption but it's been rather a stormy relationship over the years. Then recently he met his original father. Since then he seems like a different person. He is much more accepting and less judgmental. Have you heard of this happening before?

Yes, I have. It's an interesting phenomenon. It seems that some adopted people (men, in particular) find it difficult to accept that their mothers allowed them to be adopted. Somehow, hearing

35

the same story from their father makes all the difference. I always hope that mothers will be able to see that there are many benefits for all concerned in supporting their children to contact their fathers.

I've met the son that I lost to adoption but his adoptive parents were not happy about us seeing each other. They told him that he was not allowed to mention me when he was with them. So because of the tension this caused, he saw less and less of them and then they started to say that I had ruined their life and turned him away from them. Is there any way that he can get them to be more generous and understanding?

After an adoption reunion takes place, what usually happens is that the people involved become more aware of themselves and more confident in who they are. This often gives them a sense of freedom. Inevitably, this affects their relationships with other people. Once people like themselves more and understand themselves better, they relate more honestly and openly to other people. Often this means that relationships are strengthened, but not always. It seems that your son's adoptive parents feel threatened by your presence in his life. I hope that they will learn to accept that he has a place in all of his families, otherwise they may be the ones to drive him away.

I gave up two sons for adoption many years ago. I just don't know how I'm ever going to explain that either to them or to the daughter I raised. I can't quite come to terms with it myself and when I've tried to tell other people, they find it very hard to understand.

There are many parents who have lost more than one child to adoption. The factors which were operating at that time are often complex. It's possible that there was a degree of loyalty to the first child, that would not allow you to raise the second. If adoption was presented to you as being 'the right thing to do' for your first child then why would it not also be 'right' for your second child? It's probable that little, if anything, had changed in your circumstances, to persuade you to think any differently. It shows how powerful the forces in favour of adoption were at that time, that you could have been persuaded to repeat the procedure. It's also very likely that you had not grieved the loss of the first child and were really not in a healthy emotional state to be dealing with a second pregnancy. There was also a familiarity about consenting to adoption, because you had experienced it already. When we're under stress, our behaviour tends to revert to familiar patterns. Losing a child to adoption often results in low self-esteem, because of the guilt and shame involved. If you were feeling worthless after the loss of your first child, then how could you be expected to have the confidence that you could raise a second child competently? I'm sure there were many contributing factors which led to this outcome for you. It would be useful for you to explore them, perhaps with professional help, in order that you can accept and understand your experience and then you will be more comfortable sharing it with others, including your children.

I gave up my daughter for adoption many years ago, because I was told that it was the 'right' thing to do. Then later I was blamed for not raising her myself. I'm confused now. Did I do the 'right' thing? Would I still have been blamed if I had done the 'wrong' thing?

I think many mothers in the past found themselves in a 'no-win' situation in which there was no 'right' choice. They had no way of knowing what the long term impact of their decisions would be. Adoption was presented as the 'right' thing to do because it was felt to be in the best interests of their children. They were often made to feel that raising their children would be selfish. I believe that by becoming pregnant when they did, they challenged the expectations of society at the time and so others tried to make them feel inferior and inadequate. I hope that single parents today recognise that their freedoms were largely built upon the sufferings of others in earlier decades.

Since our reunion, my daughter has made it very clear that her adoptive parents are much more important to her than I am. She rarely contacts me and seems to expect me to be grateful for the small amount of time she condescends to share with me. I'm finding this more and more hurtful as time goes on and I'm wondering if it would be better for me not to see her at all, rather than being constantly reminded that she clearly considers me second-rate compared to her adoptive parents. Would I be wise to break off all contact with her?

> *Your feelings are not uncommon. It might be helpful for you to spell out your feelings to your daughter (perhaps in a letter) clearly and without blame. You may want to reassure your daughter that you care about her and want her to be a part of your life, but that certain aspects of the current situation are making you feel unhappy. You run the risk, of course, of alienating your daughter and then not hearing from her at all. Only you can decide if the situation is such that you are prepared to take that risk. As family members, we each have our role to play but there is not always agreement on what that role will be. Remember too that in families where there has been no adoption, parents are sometimes dissatisfied with the amount of time allocated to them by their adult children. Once our children become adults, they lead their own lives and make their own decisions. Where there has been an adoption-related separation, of course, the issues are more complex because the expectations of both parties to the reunion might be quite different. Sometimes adopted children like to feel that they are able to control the degree of contact with their original parents and this may be what is happening with your daughter. There are many parents who don't even know if their children are alive or dead and there are*

others whose children refuse any contact at all. Perhaps you might find more contentment if you are able to enjoy the contact that you have with your daughter without being disappointed that you do not have more of her time.

I'm the father of a child who was given up for adoption. I never saw my daughter when she was born and yet I thought about her and missed her for thirty years, before I finally contacted her. Does that surprise you?

Not at all – in fact it seems perfectly normal that a parent would continue to care about their child, regardless of the lack of contact between them. Parents who are separated from their children by divorce, for example, continue to care about their children. I'm delighted that you were able to let your daughter know that you cared for her and hadn't forgotten her.

All through the years that I didn't know what had become of my son, I thought about him all the time. However, his birthday was always the most difficult day for me. Now that I've met him, I still find myself feeling sad on his birthday. I don't want to spoil the day for him. Have you any suggestions to help me?

Many original parents find it helpful, whether they have been reunited with their children or not, to set aside some time on their child's birthday to honour their parenthood and their feelings for their child. This can be useful for adopted people also, as they may feel a degree of sadness on their birthdays. Their birthday, after all, is an annual reminder that they were not raised with the families into which they were born. Some people light a candle, or bake a cake. Some write a statement or a poem. Some recognise the significance of the day in their journal. You can be creative and invent your own form of ritual to mark the occasion. If those affected by adoption separation can deliberately set aside a time early in the day to acknowledge their experience and their

39

loss, then it is more likely that they will be able to approach the remaining part of the day with a positive attitude.

When I was reunited with my son, my parents wanted to meet him too. I was really upset and didn't want to share him with them, especially when they were the ones who made me give him away in the first place. Do you think they deserve to meet him?

For many original mothers and sometimes also fathers, their anger with their parents resurfaces at the time of reunion. Looking back, it seems to many that their parents were harsh and judgmental and could have done more to help keep the child within the family circle. However, if adult adopted children can be generous enough to understand the position their original parents were in when they were born, I think the original parents can try to understand how it was for their own parents. It might be helpful to your healing if you spoke to your parents and tried to understand their motives and intentions at the time your son was born. Hopefully you can work through some of your anger, so that your son can benefit from what your parents have to offer him.

I decided to try to find the son I gave up for adoption, but by the time I managed to trace him he was already dead. I am devastated and angry and feel as if I've lost him twice. I felt guilty before about giving him up, but now I feel even more guilty. Perhaps I should have looked for him sooner. Perhaps his death had something to do with the fact that I didn't raise him. How can I ever deal with my grief when the possibility of reunion has been denied me?

This is a tragic outcome and I am very sorry that you have lost your son. There are no easy answers to your question. I believe that insightful counselling could help you to come to terms with the circumstances which led to the adoption. Also your anger is quite appropriate, but I believe it is important that you don't turn it inwards on yourself. Perhaps you can find a way to 'get to

40

know' your son through the people who did know him. Is it possible for you to have some memento of him or to visit his grave? It might be useful for you to have copies of his birth and death certificates to allow you to confront the reality that he existed. Perhaps you could create your own ritual to acknowledge his death and your motherhood. You are not responsible for your son's death and I hope that you will find someone supportive who can help you to manage your grief.

So many adopted people seem to express a lot of anger towards their original mothers and/or fathers. Is it mostly the ones who have had negative experiences in their adoptive families who react in this way?

Hostility is a common component of grief, which often comes to the surface during adoption reunions. Many adopted people are angry and many of them direct that anger towards their original mothers and also sometimes towards other family members. In my experience, many adopted people who display intense hostility towards members of their families of origin also claim to have had a happy upbringing in their adoptive families. Sometimes the way they express their anger is by refusing contact with their original parents. If adopted people can explore and understand why they are so angry, this can improve their level of emotional well-being, as well as helping them to build relationships with family members.

I am a father who lost a child through adoption. I recently met my son and was horrified to be told by him that he was abused by his adoptive parents and removed from their home under child protection legislation. We were told that adoptive parents would give our child all the advantages which we were unable to give him. How could this be allowed to happen?

Yours is a tragic story. Some parents, adoptive or otherwise, do not have the skills and the commitment to be able to raise children competently. Adoptive parenting is particularly demanding owing to the impact on the child of being separated from their original families. It is heartbreaking for original parents to discover that their children did not, in fact, receive all of the expected advantages in their adoptive families. Hopefully you can now have some positive input into your son's life and help him to heal the hurts from the past.

I was told by a social worker that the daughter I gave up for adoption wants to contact me. I'm fifty-two years old and I have a good husband who loves me dearly but I've never told him about that child. How can I tell him that I've lied all these years? I just couldn't face the past coming back into my life now. Surely at my age I should be protected from this kind of thing?

It must have been a terrible strain for you to keep your daughter a secret for all those years and it may not be easy to acknowledge her existence now. In fact, she has never been in the past, as you have carried the thought of her with you for many years. Imagine what a relief it could be to be honest finally and to release yourself from the tension of hiding the fact that you had a child who was adopted. Secrets are corrosive and destructive in relationships because people are not living with reality – instead they are trying to avoid it. It's wonderful that your daughter wants to know you and this is a great opportunity for you to express your feelings and be true to your motherhood. 'Protecting' yourself from the truth in a situation like this is actually condemning yourself to on-going deceit and stress. You may find that your husband will be relieved to know the truth, as he may have been aware of your reactions to certain events over the years, for which he had no explanation. Adoption reunions often raise deep emotions for those involved and it's a time when you need the support of those who love you. If you and your husband have a close relationship, then I'm sure that he will continue to love you and that he will be happy to support you in your reunion with your daughter. If he really loves you, then he'll love you for who you are, not just who he thought you were. I'm sure he will appreciate that you have trusted him enough to give him a realistic picture of who you are, one which includes the fact that you have a daughter. It may not be easy in the beginning, but once you have faced the truth, I'm sure you'll wonder what it was that you feared so much.

I wrote to my son but he didn't write back. I waited three months and then wrote again, but there was still no response. I know he's living there because I have a friend who knows the family. Don't you think he at least owes it to me to let me know that he's alive and has received my letters?

I don't think adoption reunions are about people 'owing' anything to each other. I don't see it as being about obligation. Legally he doesn't owe you anything, although some people might think he has a moral obligation to you. If he chooses to respond to you, then I'm sure you'll be delighted. Many people are not prepared for contact and it takes some time before they are ready to respond. I hope that you can be patient with him and not give up. He may be dealing with other issues in his life at this time, of which you are unaware. You have offered him a great opportunity, but he may not be ready at this stage of his life to accept your offer graciously. In the meantime, you can work on taking care of your own recovery, regardless of his behaviour.

I've been reunited with my daughter but she's been terribly spoilt and expects to be treated like a princess. I'm sure she wouldn't have been so selfish and self-centred if I had raised her. Why did this happen?

Sometimes adoptive parents have tried to compensate for the fact that their adopted children have been separated from their original families. By doing so, they may have, in fact, prevented the child from growing and developing in the way that most of us do, by dealing with adversity and learning to be resilient. As a result some adopted children have grown up expecting to receive everything they want with little effort on their part and are not well prepared for life's challenges. On the other hand, studies with identical twins separated at birth suggest that their inherent personalities have had more impact on their lives than the environments in which they were raised. You'll never know how much of your daughter's behaviour is a result of her personality and how much is a result of her upbringing. While, to some extent, it would make it easier to build a relationship if you are able to accept her for who she is, I think it would also be appropriate for you to discuss with her what it is about her behaviour that concerns you and to set your own boundaries.

We married after giving up our son for adoption. We met him again when he was eighteen years old and he was surprised to find that he resembled our other children. This puzzled us as it seemed natural to us that our children would look alike. Can you explain this?

It's sometimes difficult to understand the degree of denial that exists in some adoption situations. Some adopted children grow up absorbing denial to such an extent that a thirty-year-old adopted man I spoke to was worried about his hair loss, because his adoptive father was bald at an early age. One adopted woman said that she did not expect her original mother to be short like her, as everyone in her adoptive family was tall. These people are living in an unhealthy fantasy world with an astonishing degree of denial. They may have acquired these attitudes because of the community denial that surrounds adoption.

I gave up a daughter for adoption. She was conceived as a result of a rape experience. I thought that I had put the experience behind me, but then I got a letter when she was thirty years old saying that she wanted to contact me. I saw a counsellor over a period of some months and found the counselling very useful. I hadn't realised that I needed to grieve the loss of my child. Finally I felt that I was prepared for meeting my daughter. However she has been very rude and angry towards me since we met and now I wish that I had never met her. I know I can't go back and change what has happened, but I feel that, as long as I told myself she was probably happy and had had a good upbringing, then I was able to live with it all. Now I find that the thought of her and the way she behaved towards me just makes me unhappy. I feel that it would have been better for me if the meeting had never taken place. How can I learn to live with what has happened?

I can understand that it has been very painful for you to have been subjected to your daughter's anger and resentment. It's unfortunate that she behaved in that way towards you. However, the fact that she did contact you drew your attention to your need for support in your grieving and this has been very useful to you. While it may have felt more comfortable, in some ways, to have held on to the fantasy of how your daughter's life might have turned out, you are now forced to deal with the reality. While you have to accept her as a person, you do not have to accept her rudeness. Many adopted people are angry, as are many original parents, but there is no justification for expressing that anger in hurtful ways towards a family member. I suggest that you express clearly to your daughter that you love her and care about her, but stress that you expect to be treated politely by her and make sure that, as the parent, you model the type of behaviour which you would like her to exhibit. Hopefully your daughter will also seek appropriate help and find ways to explore and express her feelings, which do not involve insulting and hurting other people. As you say, you cannot turn back the clock. The reunion has been a great opportunity for both of you to address the issues which the adoption separation has brought to your lives. You can make sure that you make the most of that opportunity, but you cannot dictate how your daughter will use her opportunities. Please be patient, remember that you are the parent and don't give up hope that she will grow in understanding and compassion.

I understand how I was not able to grieve the loss of my child, at the time he was adopted, because of the complications surrounding my grieving experience. Do you think if mothers like me had had community support at the time and been able to grieve, that everything would have been fine?

It seems to me that those women who did get some help at the time of the separation from their children and were able to grieve to some extent have shown fewer on-going signs of repressed grief. However, because of the lack of finality of the loss, I believe that it was not possible for most mothers to complete the grieving tasks at the time of separation, in the way that they may have done following a death. The reunion experience provides a type of finality and I believe that this is part of the motivation to seek to have a reunion. Also I believe that parents don't really know what it is that they have lost until their children are adults and so there is an element of the grieving which cannot be addressed early in the separation. The bottom line is that I don't believe that there is any painless way to separate parents and children.

When I was a teenager, my girlfriend and I had a baby girl and, because we were so young, our parents decided that it would be better for the baby to be adopted. I just went along with it, but, over the years, I have felt very guilty for not standing by my child's mother. When our daughter reached adulthood, I decided that it would be a good idea to get in touch with her original mother, so that, if our daughter contacted us, we would have had a chance to sort out our own differences first. We met and I was able to apologise to her. However, I realised that I still had feelings for the woman who was my childhood sweetheart, although I am now happily married. Am I just fantasising or is it possible that I married the wrong woman? Is it too late to do something about it? Does this happen often?

I do know that this does happen sometimes. Any kind of reunion which is connected with an adoption is an emotional experience and those involved can be very vulnerable. A reunion such as yours can cause the emotions which were experienced around the time of the pregnancy and birth to resurface. Sometimes there has been a great deal of anger within the original mother and/or father, which has simmered for many years. This can erupt at the time of reunion. Sometimes there was a great deal of affection between the original mother and father and that too may have continued to exist, although deeply buried, for a long time. Finally confronting the impact of the adoption separation experience can cause those warm, affectionate feelings to come to the surface. It may be that your relationship with your daughter's mother was prevented from running its course and so you have a sense that it was unnaturally broken off and remains somehow incomplete. Just be aware that this is a time of deep emotional turmoil and not a time to be making important decisions. Many original parents feel that they have not truly been themselves since the separation from their child and reliving that experience can bring a great sense of relief. This can cause some original parents to behave recklessly. Rather than making rash decisions, I would suggest that you find someone independent and trustworthy with whom you can discuss your feelings and adopt a wait-and-see policy, until the emotional turmoil has settled somewhat.

My husband and I have recently found the son that we gave up for adoption before we were married. He tells us that he already has a mother and father and cannot bring himself to call us by those names. Is this normal? Is he in denial? How can we reach an agreement on what he should call us?

You are his original mother and father and nothing can change that. The names which we give each other do not affect the nature of our relationships. Adopted people belong in one way to their adoptive family and in another way to the families of both their mothers and their fathers. However, I'm sure that you can reach an agreement with him on the issue of naming. My advice is to discuss it with him openly and calmly and remember that you are the parents. I suggest that, for now, you be guided by your son, safe in the knowledge of your relationship to him, which cannot be affected by the titles he chooses to give you. Some people have more than one person in their lives to whom they refer as 'mother' or 'father', in the same way that I have several people in my life to whom I refer as 'son'. Also remember that your son's wishes in this respect may change over time and the best that you can do is to keep the channels of communication open and be happy that he wants to include you in his life.

After I gave up my daughter for adoption, I was treated for depression. Now I've met my daughter again and I feel that the depression is coming back. Do you think I should take medication again?

First of all, I'm not a medical person and so I don't give medical advice. I do not believe that adoption outcomes should necessarily be considered to be mental health problems, but I suggest that you discuss any health concerns you have with your doctor. However, I believe that in a lot of cases where an adoption separation occurred, genuine grieving was mistaken for depression, because professional people did not recognise the adoption separation as a loss situation. It's possible that in some cases the medication actually helped to suppress the grief and so that may explain why it seems so often to come to the surface again later in life and especially at the time of reunion. This can be true for adopted people as well as their original parents. I believe that reunion often brings up the grief which was not

48

allowed to be expressed at the time of separation and that, for that reason, being sad is often an appropriate response to an adoption reunion. Unfortunately, again, many professionals do not understand this and suggest medication for a condition which, in my opinion, is not an illness, but serves a useful purpose. Reunion also can bring up feelings of anger and when anger is turned inwards it can present as depression. Once people understand that reunion reactivates the dormant grief, they are better able to manage their emotions. A little piece of information like that can make all the difference to how we deal with the situation. My little grandson, for example, thought that I could perform magic when I was able to make his toy train carriage move without touching it. One day he'll understand about the use of magnets and know that the train moved, not because his Grandma had magical power, but because of the laws of physics.

Even though it's been two years since I met my son, I still feel anxious that he'll walk out of my life again. I couldn't bear to lose him twice. Because of my fear, I find that I often hold back when I'm talking to him, as I'm afraid of saying the wrong thing. I can never really relax. Will it always be like this?

Many parents describe that feeling of 'walking on eggshells' because of their fear of somehow offending their child and then losing contact. For most people, a time comes when they feel comfortable enough to be themselves and say what they feel, with only the usual restrictions, in terms of good manners, that we employ in our dealings with other family members. It's impossible to predict when that time might come. However, rather than put yourself through so much stress for fear of what might happen, it might be better for your general well-being to try to relax more when you are in your son's company and trust him to accept you and understand your feelings for him. The relationship will continue if you both want it to continue and it is unlikely that he would terminate it after two years on the basis of one misunderstanding or disagreement. Maybe the relationship could actually be strengthened by being tested, rather than being restricted to what feels to you like 'safe' behaviour. If you show him that you are able to accept him for himself and allow him to be honest, then you are demonstrating to him the kind of behaviour which you hope he will exhibit towards you. Only you can decide whether you would rather continue to feel so constrained, or are prepared to take the risk of being yourself and letting your son respond to you in his own way.

It's been wonderful to meet my son again, but it seems that being with him brings back all my hurt and sadness from the time he was born. It's hard to enjoy being with him when all I can feel is the pain, especially if he talks about his childhood or his adoptive family and I realise how much I have lost. Will I ever get over this and be able to enjoy spending time with my son?

I think it's vital to the future of your relationship with your son that you manage to address your sadness in ways that do not interfere with the building of this relationship. Of course, meeting your son again will bring up deep feelings of loss and grief for you. It is likely that these feelings have not been addressed and it is certainly in your best interests to explore those feelings and to experience them. However, I hope that you can find a way to do that, which is separate from the time you spend with your son, so that he does not feel that he is causing your sadness. It's not him, nor the reunion with him which is causing your hurt and sadness. It is the original separation which has caused your pain. I hope that you will find a way to work through that grief so that you can go on to enjoy fully the pleasure of having your son in your life.

I want to be more open about the daughter I lost to adoption, but I don't know how to tell people. What should I say?

50

You can practise using whichever words feel comfortable for you. You might want to bring it up when you meet a new person and they ask if you have children. People sometimes say, 'I have three children, two daughters and a son, but my son was born before I was married and I was persuaded that he would be better off if I gave him up for adoption.' Some say, 'I have three children, but I was able to raise only two of them. My first child was taken from me to be adopted.' Some say, 'I had one child, a son, but I lost him through adoption.' You can experiment and find which statements you feel represent your experience and your feelings and try them out, until eventually the information will be easy to share. Every time you talk about your child as being a part of your family and a part of your life, you are acknowledging the truth and owning your experience. You may also be educating another person and helping to increase community awareness of adoption issues.

I've never felt sad about giving up my daughter for adoption, as I think it was the best thing for everyone concerned. I don't see that I have any need to grieve. I did cry a lot after they took her away and over the years when I didn't know what had become of her, but now that I know she's had a good life, I don't think adoption is really something to grieve over. Why do you think people can benefit from grieving over something that has turned out all right?

It's interesting that you say that you didn't feel sad about the separation from your daughter and yet you shed many tears. Crying is certainly one way to grieve and possibly the most common way of expressing grief. No matter how the adoption seems to have turned out for both of you, there has been a separation of mother and child and there have been losses experienced. Many people have buried their feelings of loss and so their grief, when it does occur, takes them by surprise. Some people, however, have been able to acknowledge and express their feelings (for example by crying) and so for them much of the

51

grieving has already been accomplished, before they find out what the outcomes of the separation have been for the other party. Anecdotal evidence suggests that those who have had those opportunities to grieve cope better with reunion, because they are more prepared for it by having already addressed, to some extent, their loss issues. When your daughter was adopted, no one knew if it would 'turn out all right'. I think that the grieving is about the separation and the loss, regardless of the outcomes. It may be that if your daughter had had an unhappy life as an adopted child, then there may have been more grief for you on learning of that.

I've been reunited with my son but his wife seems to be so jealous and it seems that she would like me to disappear out of his life again. Is this normal?

It's certainly common but not what I would call 'normal'. Strong feelings occur around adoption reunion but many of them are neither healthy nor productive – nor are they in any way inevitable. However, you need to be mindful of the fact that your son may feel that his first loyalty is to his partner. In that case, it would be good for you to acknowledge that and to avoid any situation in which he might feel that he has to choose to please one or the other of you. Also, try to be patient and undemanding and allow your relationship to develop at its own pace, bearing in mind that he needs to find a place in his life for all of the people who are important to him. This is not an easy task. However, many people's lives these days are complex and they are able to manage them.

I've managed to contact my daughter, but she has refused to meet me, because she thinks it will upset her adoptive parents. I'm really angry with them for raising her to believe that she should be responsible for their comfort. How can any kind of parents encourage their adult children to deny themselves valuable opportunities, just because the parents think it would make life more complicated for them?

I know that there are many adoptive parents who have made it clear to their adopted children that they would not be happy if they had a reunion with their original parents or other relatives. However, I also know that there are many adopted adults who make their own decisions regardless. It may be hard for you to accept, but your daughter is an adult and has made her own choice. If she has really been unduly influenced by her adoptive parents, then she has allowed that to happen and, as an adult, must take responsibility for that. Hopefully she will come to see that a reunion with you would be a valuable learning experience for everyone involved.

I've met my daughter but I find it difficult to feel close to her. How is it that she seems to be so relaxed with my other children?

Relationships between siblings often lack the tension that may be present in relationships between parents and adult children who have been separated by adoption. Often that tension reduces over time. Meantime, I hope that you can enjoy and appreciate the fact that your children are close and be patient and allow your own relationship with your daughter to grow and develop at its own pace.

I've met the daughter I gave up for adoption and we get on well together. Everyone thinks I should be happy now but I still get very sad sometimes, when I think that I gave her up and was not able to be a mother to her. Will I ever get over it?

I don't think it's about 'getting over it'. Of course you will always have some sadness related to the separation from your daughter. I think that's perfectly natural. When those times arise, I suggest that you just let yourself experience those feelings and know that they will pass and that they will not prevent you from having a contented and fulfilling life. We all have events in our past which we revisit from time to time; some are sad events and some are happy ones. Just be glad that you are able to get in touch with your feelings and experience them. Expressing your feelings is not as big a problem as not being able to express them. It's a question of finding a place for those feelings in your life and not allowing them to overshadow the good feelings that you have about your daughter. Your relationship with your child will always have an element of sadness, in the same way that emigrants, no matter how much they appreciate the benefits of life in their chosen destination, often live with a sense of what has been lost. You brought her into the world and now you have her in your life. That's something to celebrate.

My son refuses to tell his children who I am, because he does not want his adoptive parents to know of our reunion. His children don't know he's adopted and think that I'm a friend of the family. I hate to see my grandchildren being raised with lies and secrets. How can I persuade him to be honest with them?

This situation is not uncommon. It's very hard to see the secrecy and deceit associated with adoption being carried through into another generation. Perhaps you could explain to your son that you value the truth and do not wish to be involved in deceit. I hope that he will see the wisdom of openness and honesty. Adopted people who do not tell their adoptive parents that they have met their original family members, are denying them the choice of whether or not to share that important experience with their child. Adoptive parents have always known that they were raising someone else's child. They have always known that there was a possibility that the child would be reunited with their families of origin, although they may have chosen not to prepare themselves or their child for that event. Are you able to discuss it with his wife? Perhaps she could talk to him about this. In the meantime if you concentrate on building a strong, close relationship with your son and his family, then when he is able to reveal the truth, you will be there to provide support.

I've been reunited with my son, but my parents refuse to meet him. Is that common?

Yes, it is common. Older people tend to be less adaptable and sometimes find it difficult to assimilate 'new' family members. Also, many grandparents were instrumental in arranging the adoptions of their grandchildren, or at least did not prevent those adoptions from taking place and so the reunion often brings up feelings of guilt and loss for them, which they sometimes wish to avoid. Hopefully their attitudes will change over time.

A few years after I lost my daughter to adoption I spent three months in a mental health facility with what was termed at the time a 'nervous breakdown'. When my daughter became an adult, I was terrified that she would want to contact me. I thought that if I had to revisit all that pain, I may have another breakdown. We met, however and I didn't have a breakdown. In fact, it has been a joyous and wonderful experience. Do you think my earlier breakdown may have actually served a purpose?

It's certainly possible that what was termed a 'nervous breakdown' was actually your way of processing your grief. It may be that when you were reunited with your daughter, the grief which arose was thereby made more manageable. I have heard of many parents who have suffered breakdowns between losing their children and being reunited with them, sometimes triggered by another loss event. Often no connection is made between the breakdown and the adoption separation, but it may well be that your grief forced itself to the surface and made you deal with it in the early days, thereby saving you from going through that degree of anguish again at the time of reunion.

My wife and I gave up our first child for adoption. The only way we could live with that decision has been to convince ourselves that we did the right thing. I'm terrified that if we try to contact our child, we might find out that we didn't do the right thing for him after all. What would you advise?

Your decision was made with good and positive intentions, but with no knowledge of what the outcomes would be. I think that you would be helping yourselves and your son to work towards resolving all of your adoption issues by making contact with him and confronting the truth.

I gave up my son for adoption and I would love to find out how he is and maybe even get to meet him. However, people are telling me that that wouldn't be fair to his adoptive parents and that I should think of them and stay out of their lives. What do you think?

Your son is an adult and he is the one you need to consider, not his adoptive parents. Many adoptive parents are delighted when their adopted children are reunited with their original families. I believe that you would be doing all of them a favour, by making a considerate approach. Your son will make his own decisions.

Why do adopted people sometimes object to their parents referring to them as their 'adopted child'?

I don't know. I have five adult children. They will always be my children, no matter how old they (or I) become. They are my sons and my daughters. Your child is your child in the same way that your mother is your mother, regardless of how old either one is. Our children become adults and then they are our adult children. The key point is, though, that parents discuss with their children how they prefer to be described and that they reach an agreement on the matter.

I know that losing a child to adoption is in some ways like experiencing a bereavement, but I also know that I dare not say that to people who have experienced the death of a child. I am afraid that they will tell me that their grief is worse than mine, because they know that they will never see their child again. Which do you think is worse, death or adoption?

I don't think it's helpful to compare the two experiences. I don't think it's possible or useful to say that one type of loss is greater or has a deeper impact than another. Everyone's losses can be acknowledged. One of the problems with adoption has been that, in the past, it was not recognised as a loss experience. We suffer many types of losses throughout our lives, through death, the ending of relationships, emigration and ill-health, among others. It's important that we educate the community to understand that parents did suffer from the loss of their children who were adopted. I believe that this is more likely to be achieved without making comparisons.

My son was not well-treated by his adoptive parents, who had very definite expectations of him, which he failed to fulfil. Yet he still seems to show a strong sense of loyalty to them. Is this common?

Yes, it is. Sometimes it seems that because adopted people felt that they had been abandoned by their original families and therefore cannot trust them, they will not dare to take the risk of alienating their adoptive families, in case they find themselves with no family at all. I met one young woman who was adopted and she was placed in an orphanage by her adoptive father after her adoptive mother died when she was five years old. She had met her original parents, but told me that her 'primary allegiance' still lay with her adoptive family. Even children who have been abused by their parents can still show a strong sense of attachment to them. I don't think it would be useful for you to challenge what he perceives as loyalty. I suggest that you concentrate on your relationship with your son and make sure that he knows that you love him unconditionally.

My son who was lost to adoption has come back into our lives but I find that my other son, whom I raised, seems to be jealous of his brother. Is this normal?

I would say it is not uncommon. It may take some time for your family to accommodate your son, who has been absent for so many years. Be patient and try to be cautious and considerate of the effort involved in adjusting to this new situation. In any family there are those who are close and those who are not. We have to accept that.

My wife and I have been reunited with the daughter we gave up for adoption before we were married. She was happy to hear from us but said that if we had left her alone, she would never have looked for us. I've heard that only a small percentage of adopted people search for their families. Is this true and if so why do you think it is? Do you think this means that the others are quite content without a reunion?

First of all, it's impossible to know how many adopted people have sought a reunion, as some do not use official assistance. Also we have no way of knowing how many were not told they were adopted or have died before reaching adulthood. Some adopted people say that they had never thought of searching but, in fact, by not searching they had, by default, made a decision not to search for their original parents. Some don't want to stir up their own buried feelings of loss. Some feel that they have nothing to offer. Some are angry with their original parents and don't want to share any part of themselves. Some fear a negative reaction from their adoptive parents. In spite of the fact that they have chosen not to take an active role in the search process, however, many adopted adults are delighted to have been contacted by their original parents.

58

I'm so ashamed of having allowed my child to be adopted. I feel that somehow I should have been able to prevent it. Will I ever get rid of this guilt?

Yes, you can. The sense of shame which so many mothers experienced came from the attitudes of others. It seems to me, looking back, that pregnancy leading to marriage was not so shameful, but pregnancy that didn't lead to marriage was usually very shameful. Apparently there were priests in Ireland who used to say that pregnancies usually last nine months, but 'first babies can come any time' (meaning any time after marriage, of course). I think that a lot of women were made to feel ashamed because they became pregnant to men who either refused to marry them or whom they did not want to marry. In order to release yourself from that shame, you can focus on the reality of your situation, try to understand how and why it happened and accept that you acted with good intentions. You can find a place in your life for your adoption experience and be proud that you are a parent and that you brought a child into the world. You can work out how to make sure that the pain from the past does not prevent you from having joy in the present.

I don't understand adoptive parents. How could they just take someone else's child? I could never do that.

How many times have you heard someone say, or dreaded hearing someone say, 'I don't understand people who gave up their children for adoption. How could anyone just give away their baby? I could never do that.'? There is nothing inherently wrong in wanting to give a child a home. Many adoptive parents believed that they were doing what was best for the children. When mothers gave consent for their children to be adopted, they were not able to predict the implications and the far-reaching consequences of that event. Adoptive parents also were not able to predict the implications for themselves and the children they were adopting, because at the time so many adoptions took place, there

59

was no reliable research available on the long term outcomes. To understand how and why so many adoptions have happened, it is useful to explore people's motives and intentions. I don't think it's useful to look for somewhere to pin the blame.

I recently found the son that I gave up for adoption. Now I suspect that he is sexually involved with my daughter (his half-sister). I'm horrified. How could this happen?

Siblings who have been raised together have usually learned that brothers and sisters are not appropriate candidates to be sexual partners. Siblings who have been raised apart, however, have not had the opportunity to absorb these attitudes towards each other and the barriers which normally grow in families do not exist between them. This is compounded by the fact that those who were adopted as children have grown up among people who do not reflect them physically and they sometimes (perhaps subconsciously) seek such people and are attracted to partners who resemble them. When they meet relatives, who do reflect them physically, they are often drawn to each other in a physical as well as an emotional way. This can also occur between parents and children. Usually, if those feelings exist, they are not acted upon. As the relationships between family members grow and develop and the initial intensity subsides, they usually come to realise that sexual behaviour such as this is inappropriate.

My son was adopted but it was an open adoption and so we had some contact over the years. I was told that this would mean that he wouldn't have the same issues which adopted people have who were raised without any contact with their original families. Now he's an adult and he tells me that he feels that he doesn't belong in either family. Do you think that the contact was of any value?

There are not enough children who have been raised with so-called 'open' adoption arrangements like these and who are now adults, for research to have been conducted which would give us any indication of the long term outcomes. From my own experience of talking with parents whose children have been raised with some contact with their families of origin, the issues for these children are very similar to the issues experienced by those who were raised without contact with their families. Mothers have told me that their children, as they approached adolescence and began to understand the position in which they found themselves, sometimes became resentful towards their original parents, whom they saw, at that stage of their lives, as being relatively mature and prosperous. These adolescents had difficulty understanding why their parents had chosen not to raise them, especially if subsequent children had been born and raised within the family. In many situations, also, arrangements for contact were made but contact ceased a short time after the adoption took place. Sometimes contact was broken off by the original parents, who found it too painful. Sometimes contact was broken off by the adoptive parents, who found it too threatening. Anecdotal evidence suggests that children raised with contact will still suffer from the loss of their position in their original families and that parents who have been separated from their children through adoption, even when they have had a degree of contact, will still suffer from the loss of their parental roles in the lives of their children.

My daughter searched for me and found me. It was a huge surprise but I was delighted that she wanted to know me. Everything went well for the first three months and then all of a sudden she turned on me, was really angry and hurtful and said that she never wanted to hear from me again. Why did she bother to look for me, if she was only going to walk out of my life again?

Adoption reunions tend to rekindle feelings of loss and grief related to the original separation. Hostility is a common component of grieving behaviour following a bereavement and so

61

is the inclination to try to escape from the truth and pretend that the death has not really happened. Similar behaviour also occurs sometimes after an adoption reunion. Your daughter may also be dealing with other issues in her life at this time, of which you are unaware. Try to be patient with her and allow her time to work through her grief. Remember too that you are the parent. She may not fully comprehend what it is that she is experiencing and may feel lost and afraid, as many people do during their grieving, whether they are grieving a death or another type of separation. She may have felt when she searched for you that she wanted to have you in her life forever, but no one can predict what they will experience after the reunion has occurred. It may not be easy, but perhaps you can find a way to reassure her of your feelings for her and at the same time allow her the opportunity to work through her own feelings. Her behaviour is common in adoption reunion experiences and many reunions survive this sort of phase. I know it's difficult to deal with, but, hopefully, if she knows she can rely on you not to give up on her, she'll move through this phase and it will become a learning experience on which both of you can build.

I am a mother who lost a child through adoption. Now that we have been reunited, my son wants to know about his father. I love my son dearly, but why should I help him to find his father now, when he abandoned me during my pregnancy and refused to take any responsibility? He caused me nothing but heartache and I don't want anything to do with him. Why doesn't my son understand how hurtful this is for me?

Adopted people have two original parents, like everyone else. Many mothers hope that their adopted children will want to know them. Why would they not want to know their fathers too? Mothers who lost children through adoption were usually young and disempowered. Many years later, when their children are adults, the mothers they are meeting have matured and grown in awareness and understanding. Mothers can exercise the same courage and generosity which their children have exhibited in being reunited with them, to give fathers the same opportunity. Hopefully your son's father has also grown in awareness and understanding over the years. Many fathers have carried the guilty burden of having abandoned the mothers of their children. Many mothers have lived with secrecy, stress and denial, not facing reality. They would be doing the child's father a favour by releasing him from the same experiences. They would also be doing their children a great favour if they can help them to locate their fathers. I think your son, as an adult, is entitled to make his own choice with regard to a relationship with his father, just as you are. You risk alienating your son if you try to prevent the possibility of such a relationship by withholding information.

I've been sending my daughter a birthday card and Christmas card every year for five years and have never had a response. Should I give up?

I have heard of adopted people who were delighted to receive such correspondence, even though they have never responded to it. At least you are able to write to her and she has accepted your mail. Many parents are unable to do even this. Because of your efforts, your daughter can never deceive herself into thinking that you don't care about her and hopefully one day she will respond in some way. I hope you won't give up.

I'm a father who recently was reunited with my daughter, who was given up for adoption twenty years ago. I'm really sad about all the years we've missed spending together and angry at the way my feelings were disregarded when she was born. My daughter, however, seems to be very cool. She never talks about her feelings or tells me that she cares about me. I find it very hard to connect with her. What do you think she's experiencing? Are things likely to change?

It's impossible to know how much of your daughter's behaviour reflects her personality and how much of it is a result of the impact of adoption separation in her life. Many adopted people are cautious and fear abandonment. As a result they tend to be undemonstrative and to avoid commitment. This is their way of protecting themselves against what they might perceive as a rejection. It would be helpful for you to read about the impact of adoption on adopted people, as this might help you to understand her better. Remember also that people show their feelings in different ways and be glad that she is obviously keen to spend time with you. Try to be patient with her as she is young and her attitude may change as she matures. Also it would be useful for you to be able to explore your own feelings around the adoption and to manage them in a way that does not interfere with the relationship with your daughter.

My son was conceived through rape. I've considered searching for him just to find out if he's all right, but I'm terrified that he will have turned out to be like his father or that if I meet him it will bring back the horror of my rape experience. Do you think I'd be better to leave well alone?

From my experience, children conceived through rape are just as precious to their mothers as children conceived in other circumstances. Your son is a unique individual and not just the product of a disempowering, abusive event. It would probably help if you first of all work through the issue of having experienced a rape with someone who specialises in that area and then work at understanding your responses to the adoption separation, before you take the step of trying to contact your son.

I've met my son but I feel guilty, because I don't like him. He is selfish and irresponsible and I find it very hard to relate to him. However I adore his children and it's been great to develop a relationship with them. How can I learn to accept him as he is?

There are many parents who don't approve of their children's behaviour, whether they raised them or not. Perhaps you can focus on the fact that you want what's best for your son and continue to try to encourage him to make the most of his opportunities in life. It's wonderful that you are able to be part of your grandchildren's lives and hopefully you can have a good influence on them and enjoy the time spent with them. You would not have had that if the reunion had not occurred.

I've met the child that I gave up for adoption but I've never been sure who the father was. I've told my daughter that I can't remember anything about her father, because I am too embarrassed to admit that there are two possible candidates. I only want to protect my child from being hurt. Do you think I've done the right thing?

Perhaps some counselling would help you to explore your behaviour in the light of the judgmental attitudes of the time, when double standards created a lot of shame and guilt for women around their sexual behaviour. Your daughter may suspect that you are lying to her and this could have a negative impact on your relationship with her. However, only you can decide if you feel ready to be honest with her.

I am the father of a child who was lost to adoption. My name was not on the original birth certificate but I would like to know my child. Is there anything I can do?

In some situations fathers are entitled to be given identifying information about their children. Your first step might be to contact the government authority or adoption agency involved and find out what your rights are. You may even be able to have your name added to the original birth certificate. Another option might be to contact the child's mother and see if she would be willing to assist you. I hope that you are able to make yourself known to your child and that your child appreciates your efforts.

I've had a wonderful experience of reunion with my daughter. However, when I read of children adopted from foreign countries, I worry about their original mothers and how they are going to cope with losing their children. Does anyone care about them?

Sadly, there are now many cases of kidnapping, child-trafficking and exploitation of families in so-called 'third world' countries. We may never know the damage that has been caused to those mothers, families and communities. Sometimes children are treated as commodities and go to the highest bidder, leaving much suffering behind. We can only hope to educate those in the more affluent countries to think about how they can assist those needy families and communities in more ethical ways.

I decided that it was time I started to tell people about my daughter and thought that it would be wise for me first of all to try to understand how and why the adoption happened and the impact it may have had on both of our lives. I managed to read lots of books about adoption. However I found that many of them were very directive, telling me what I 'should' be feeling and doing. Not only that, but they often contradicted each other. How can people work out which books are the best ones to read?

I understand exactly what you mean. It can certainly be helpful to read of the experiences and opinions of others, but I would look very carefully at the credentials of the authors you choose. Some authors do not have a deep understanding of the dynamics of adoption separation and reunion and may completely misunderstand and therefore misrepresent what is happening. I encourage people to read as much as they can, but also to try to rely on their own judgment more than anyone else's. Be very wary of any author who tells you what you 'should' be doing or feeling or what you 'must' do. Remember that each adoption experience is unique and try to find perspectives that feel right for you. Part of the reason I wrote my own books was because of my personal dissatisfaction with many of the books available about adoption.

66

Personal Recovery

1. What is personal recovery?

The effects of adoption separation on individuals

Adoption separation causes an emotional trauma for those affected and I believe that an emotional *recovery* will help to heal the pain of the losses associated with adoption separation. The connection between the physical body and the emotional self is complex. I have often witnessed how people's physical well-being improves as they begin to address their emotional issues. The two are closely intertwined and in the same way that physical pain indicates that an area of the body needs treatment, so emotional pain indicates that there are issues which require attention, in order that we can recover and feel emotionally well again. I have termed this 'personal recovery'. *Personal recovery is about addressing the effects of adoption separation on individuals.*

Because the grief associated with adoption separation has been disenfranchised, those affected have often buried their grief and have therefore not processed it by going through the phases and tasks of mourning. I believe that this explains why those who have been separated from a family member by adoption seek to achieve a personal recovery, by exploring the significance of their adoption experience. In my view, they have a subconscious desire to move through the mourning process in relation to the loss created by the adoption separation and to reach a state of 'reorganised behaviour' and 'move on with life'.

If you decide to undertake personal recovery work, you are aiming to explore the experience of adoption separation, to understand it and acknowledge it and to validate your feelings about it. Personal recovery takes place on two levels. On an intellectual level, you are aiming to understand what happened and on an emotional level, you are aiming to get in touch with how you feel about what happened. The recovery process can be enhanced by attending an appropriate support group and by reading books about adoption.

I believe that for those separated from a family member by adoption, their feelings of sadness and grief are actually the expected outcome of having experienced a loss which has often been unacknowledged or misunderstood. Acknowledging the loss can be the first step towards enjoying a more contented and productive life. Because personal recovery work is a part of the adoption grieving process, however, the process itself can give rise to intense emotional reactions.

Many original parents are deterred from acknowledging the loss of their child by feelings of guilt and shame. These can be reduced by exploring the historical and social context of the circumstances which led to the adoption. Many adopted adults are deterred from acknowledging the loss of their original families by negative community attitudes. They can learn to see their adoption in a more honest light, by confronting the reality of what it has meant for them to be separated from their original families. It can be very helpful to adopted people to have information about the circumstances in the lives of both their original parents and their adoptive parents which led up to the adoption.

Why undertake personal recovery work?
Personal recovery can be very valuable for both adopted adults and their original parents. It is a way of freeing up any energy that has been tied up in suppressing their grief. After a degree of personal recovery has been achieved, that energy can then be used to move forward with healing. If personal recovery work is not undertaken, then those affected by adoption separation can remain locked in denial and the anxiety which results from it.

One of the reasons for undertaking personal recovery work is to learn to live with the loss. Although the losses caused by adoption separation may have been painful, it is not productive for those involved to have an unhealthy attachment to their pain. They can learn to celebrate their survival instead of apologising for it.

70

Because family members separated by adoption may have assumed from the attitudes of others that their feelings of loss and grief resulting from the separation were not valid, they have often lost trust in their own emotions. I believe that we are all born with a sense of self-preservation which assists us, if it is supported and allowed to develop, to make choices and judgments which are in our best interests. Because their judgment was challenged at the time of adoption separation, many original parents lost trust in that ability to care for themselves. I believe that there is a link to the inner self which can be seriously damaged by the adoption separation and that, from that time on, many struggle to reconnect with that protective inner voice. The result is that, after an adoption separation, many have made choices which were not in their best interests.

I have come to believe, however, that that damaged connection can be repaired. I have witnessed that repair happen many times. If those who have been separated from a family member by adoption can feel the sense of loss connected to that separation, express their grief and know that those emotions are valid and appropriate, then they can experience a degree of healing. This can allow them to renew their acquaintance with that innate sense of judgment. They can, in fact, rewrite the script which they learned from others, who told them that their feelings were inappropriate. They are then better able to make choices which will genuinely be in their best interests, because they will be allowing themselves to experience authentic emotions.

Personal recovery work can be undertaken at any time after the adoption separation, but original parents generally find that their feelings mature as their children mature. Anecdotal evidence suggests that, for parents, a change in attitude to their adoption experience often takes place when their adopted children reach adulthood. This is probably because the original parent is able to consider that the possibility of forming an adult relationship with their child now exists. Even if a degree of personal recovery work has been undertaken while the child is still a minor, therefore, it can be helpful to revisit that work once the child becomes an adult. Adopted people may have grown up in families where their issues of loss and grief were recognised and acknowledged. However, they too will benefit from taking responsibility for their own personal recovery work and addressing those issues when they reach adulthood.

It is helpful for those affected by adoption separation to understand that they are entitled to grieve. I believe that their grief will always be with them and that it is up to them to choose how to address that fact. If they try to repress and deny their grief, it may force its way into their lives, in ways that can be uncomfortable and distressing. I believe that this is sometimes what has happened when a 'nervous breakdown' has occurred. If they do not take an active part in addressing their grief, there is also the danger that it will engulf them and prevent them from enjoying a productive life. This situation has sometimes been diagnosed as chronic depression. Both of these outcomes are disempowering and undesirable.

If you have been separated from a family member by adoption, it is important for you to recognise that your grief can be managed and incorporated into your life. The feeling of anger and the sense of loss associated with this grief will vary in intensity at different times in your life. Many people talk about the personal recovery process as a kind of 'thawing out' which allows the grief to come to the surface and be experienced.

Outcomes

Because adoption separation creates a loss which is difficult to grieve, undertaking personal adoption recovery work can make you feel better about yourself. It can help you to have a deeper understanding of the events of your past and to change how you think about what has happened in your life. Although you cannot change what happened in the past, you can achieve a sense of control in the present and a feeling of empowerment which can help you to move forward with a positive attitude into the future.

When you decide that the time has come to address your adoption grief, you can begin your personal recovery process by expressing what the experience of adoption separation has been like for you. You may choose first of all to write your story for yourself. Afterwards you may want to share it with a close friend or family member, discuss it with a counsellor, or explore it in a group setting. Many people prefer to express their story in artwork or music rather than in words. It is up to you to decide what method will be most useful to you. Some people tell their story in one way and then later tell it again using another medium.

Revisiting your loss may bring back memories of the part that other people played in your adoption experience. You may wish to approach them and try to resolve any outstanding issues with them. However, we are each responsible for our own healing, regardless of whether other people are willing to acknowledge the part that they played. It may be helpful for you to share your healing with others, but it is important to remember that no one else is responsible for your accommodation of your loss.

Choosing to undergo a process of personal recovery is a positive, productive decision, which shows that you are aware of the need to attend to your adoption issues in order to move forward. Taking this step is a sign of emotional strength. Telling your story will lead to healing and understanding, to renewed courage and increased generosity of spirit. If adoption has left people with only bitterness and sorrow, they have failed to grasp the opportunities which life has offered them through their adoption experiences. Adoption experiences also help people to have compassion for the tribulations of others and to put life's other challenges into perspective.

2. Exploring adoption separation

Re-grief therapy and adoption

The process of re-grief therapy involves reworking, at a later time, a loss which had not been satisfactorily resolved. It has two goals; to understand why mourning was not completed in the past (operating on an intellectual level) and to help those affected to experience their grieving emotions in the present (operating on an emotional level). During the course of re-grief therapy people's 'frozen emotions are stimulated and reawakened'. As with regular grief therapy, the outcome of re-grief therapy is an increase in self-esteem and a decrease in guilt, as well as an increase in positive feelings about the lost person (Raphael, 1983, pp385-6).

I have chosen to apply re-grief therapy to reworking an adoption loss. In the case of adoption loss, I believe that, in order to understand the reasons why the mourning was not completed, it is important to understand first of all how and why the loss occurred. An informed exploration of the circumstances leading to the separation often results in the griever having more positive feelings about their adoption experience.

Exploring these issues can be instrumental in bringing the pain and grief to the surface and it can then be experienced. Pain is not necessarily a negative outcome and preventing people from experiencing pain is not always in their best interests. Pain is not always avoidable and it is sometimes necessary in order to produce something new. Childbirth, for example, is rarely accomplished without pain.

When people can understand the basis of their pain, they are in a better position to manage it. Patients would not feel confidence in a doctor, for example, who wrote a prescription for pain relief medication rather than first of all seeking the cause of the pain. Pain is a message that there is an area that needs attention. Experiencing the pain created by adoption separation can, in fact, be a way of creating a renewed sense of self.

Anger is a common response to a loss and frequently occurs with regard to adoption loss. Many people are angry that an adoption took place, but this does not necessarily mean that they are angry with any particular person. Re-grief therapy may cause suppressed anger to come to the surface. Anger can be destructive if it results in vindictiveness and cruel accusations. Anger can, however, be a productive and helpful emotion when it is understood and managed. It may be appropriate to talk to those involved in the adoption about one's anger so that there is openness and honesty in those relationships. Telling someone about your anger is very different from expressing your anger towards that person.

Because adoption separation is a profound experience and because the emotions attached to it have often been buried for many years, re-grief therapy can itself be an emotionally traumatic process. It is wise therefore, to prepare oneself for such an undertaking and to remember that no matter how difficult it may seem, this process can lead to a personal recovery from the trauma of adoption separation. It takes courage to begin this process but the rewards can be great.

Telling your story

In the endeavour to recover, the telling of your story has enormous therapeutic value, as it can unlock your grief in order that it can be experienced. Telling your story involves exploring, examining and considering exactly what happened, how it happened, why it happened and how you felt when it happened. If you are a parent who has lost a child to adoption, telling your story involves looking at what happened long before the adoption separation event and also at what happened long after the event. If you are an adopted person, telling your own story of what has happened since your adoption can be supplemented with any information you are able to gather from your original and/or adoptive parents about what happened before your birth.

Hopefully, as you tell your story, you will begin to see connections between the events and emotions which surrounded the adoption separation. Eventually a clearer picture will emerge for you of exactly how and why it all came about. When you decide to tell your story, make sure that you choose to do so in a manner which gives you a sense of control. Pace yourself and move at a rate which suits you. If you can, set aside time to tell your story – a time in your life, a time in your day. Be prepared for the intrusion of life's crises but do not be distracted from your goal. Try to choose a time for your story when life will not be placing too many other demands on you. Telling your story will itself be demanding and will use up much of your physical and emotional energy.

Adoption has, for many people, been associated with shame, secrecy and deceit. Releasing yourself from those negative constraints will bring with it an enormous sense of relief. Freedom from secrecy is always beneficial and it is never too late in your life to achieve that. Think of what you are doing if you choose to live in a situation of deceit. By deceiving others, you are not 'protecting' them, you are actually disempowering them and possibly preventing growth and development. It is never too late to learn that lesson and to give another person the gift of being able to confront the truth.

The purpose of this exploration is not to apportion blame, not to justify or make excuses, nor is it to decide whether actions were right or wrong. Its purpose is to assist you to make links and connections between your life events and the values, beliefs and motives that give them meaning. For many whose lives are affected by adoption separation, telling their story in this way is the first time that certain patterns have become obvious and this often leads to empowering moments of clarity and acceptance and to a reduction in feelings of guilt and shame.

When you recall events in your life which were hurtful, rather than seeking someone to blame, you can gain from those experiences by focussing on what you have learned from them. If, on the other hand, you focus on yourself as having been a victim, you may be blocking your own personal development.

You may have had certain views of the events of the past and certain feelings about them, but some feelings are not helpful or productive. You cannot change events which have already happened in your life, but you can change how you think about those events and that can lead to changes in how you feel about them.

Looking after yourself

Be prepared for intense feelings to come to the surface while you tell your story. Acknowledge them and accept them. They are yours and they are legitimate. Feel them and own them. You may even experience dreams or flashbacks. Events and conversations, which you had buried, may come to the surface. Bear in mind that you may be vulnerable during this time and be careful to protect yourself.

If you can, try to factor in physical activities such as outdoor walks while you tell your story. You will gain in many ways. You will expend the energy that might arise as a result of tapping into some hidden anger. You will be able to relax and recover from the distress of reliving traumatic events. You will also be in touch with the natural world and be renewed and energised by that.

3. Re-grief therapy

Re-grief therapy model pregnancy and childbirth

This re-grief therapy programme was developed for mothers who have been separated from their children by adoption. Much of the work which I am suggesting, however, applies also to fathers. The programme can also be used by adults who were adopted as children. For them, personal recovery is about exploring honestly, without guilt or shame, what it has meant to them to grow up in an adoptive situation. This will include attitudes in the community towards adoptive families as well as the adopted person's emotional response to knowing that they were adopted and how this may have changed over the years. The experiences of the original and/or adoptive parents, if they are available, can be included as background information. This programme, based on Raphael's description of re-grief therapy, can serve as a model on which individual programmes could be constructed.

Social history

In most places, attitudes to motherhood have changed enormously over the last century, although we must not forget that in some parts of the world women are still being beaten and even killed because of the shame of an out-of-wedlock pregnancy. While there have always been some who have believed in the value of a child being raised within the family of origin, those who did not have argued for mothers and their children to be separated. Many genuinely believed that children would be disadvantaged if not raised by a married couple and sometimes mothers who were widowed or 'deserted' (ie a married woman whose husband had left her) and who had young children were encouraged to allow their children to be raised by married couples. Many single mothers, whether unmarried, widowed or 'deserted', were unable to provide for a child at a time when there was very little financial help from governments.

78

In some situations which resulted in adoption, the pregnancy was planned, but before the birth occurred the circumstances changed. More often the pregnancy was unplanned. When the pregnancy was confirmed, the expectant parents then had to consider their options. For some, marriage made the pregnancy more socially acceptable. The remaining mothers found themselves giving birth as single women. In some situations, the father of the child not only promised support but also fulfilled his promise. In others the parents of the mother provided the support. For the remainder, adoption was frequently the outcome.

In some cases, mothers did not tell their families that they had given birth. In many families, reputation and standing in the community were important and an unmarried, pregnant daughter could bring shame on the whole family. In fact, there are situations where mothers suicided rather than reveal the shame of an out-of-wedlock pregnancy. Many mothers who lost their children to adoption report that they had attempted or considered suicide, in order to prevent bringing shame on themselves and/or their families.

Sometimes the mother found herself alone and felt that she could not withstand the pressure from professionals to consent to adoption. In these cases, it is interesting to consider why those mothers were alone and vulnerable. If they had belonged to a family in which they felt that they and their child were valued, they may not have found themselves in that position. They could have had a family member, or perhaps the father of the child, with them, to prevent their exploitation.

Sometimes the decision was not made by either of the parents of the child, but by their parents or by authority figures such as doctors, ministers of religion or social workers, who believed that the child would be better off in another family. Of course, no one could have known whether or not this would be the outcome of the adoption decision.

Family values

If you were separated from your child by adoption, it is useful for you to consider that, as we grow up, we absorb the values and belief systems in which we are raised, although, later in life, there may come a time when we decide to challenge them. During adolescence, however, the value system of the family in which we are raised has an enormous impact on our own priorities and decision-making. So too do the values and standards of our peer group. It also helps to consider the beliefs and traditions of the cultural or social group to which your parents belonged, as well as the bigger picture of the historical events and movements which were occurring at the time in question.

It is helpful to explore the history of your parents, the values with which they were raised and the historical period in which their own belief systems developed. In some families, religion has been a directing force. In some families war and immigration have been factors. It is interesting to explore the growth of the relationship between your parents. How did they meet? Did their parents approve of the relationship? Were they in some way pressured into marriage? Some mothers have discovered that their own parents married because of an unplanned pregnancy. If this resulted in an unhappy marriage which was the subject of regret, then those parents may have had fears for their children finding themselves in a similar situation.

In many social groups only two choices were presented by parents to their children who were facing an out-of-wedlock pregnancy – marriage or adoption. If the parents had their own reasons not to promote a hasty marriage, this family may have been supportive of adoption. In some social and cultural groups, however, it would have been unthinkable for a child to be raised outside of the family. In those cases, adoption would not have been presented as an appropriate outcome and support would have been provided for the child to be raised within the family group.

Explore your childhood and your childhood experiences. It is important for you to understand the meaning of those experiences for you and how you felt as a child. Consider issues such as communication, or lack of it, in your family, your feelings of self-worth, approval-seeking behaviour, religious and cultural influences, the relationship between your parents, relationships with siblings, gender issues, your sense of security and safety as a child, family expectations and priorities. Think about any major changes and losses which occurred in your childhood. Perhaps there were changes in the family members; deaths, divorces, people moving away. Perhaps there were changes of environment; new homes, new schools, new countries. All of those can have a significant impact in the life of a child.

Then think about your adolescent years, how the changes of puberty were approached in your family, moral standards and expectations during the era in which you were a teenager, your role models and your first romantic experiences. Again, the emphasis is on how you experienced this period in your life and the impact that it had on your sense of your own value. Consider whether or not you feel that you had a need for approval at this period in your life, whose approval was important to you and why this might have been.

Next, consider the relationship between you and the person who became the father of the child who was lost to adoption. Some mothers were raped, some were taken advantage of by older partners, some had become what was viewed at the time as promiscuous, perhaps as a result of previous sexual abuse and some were involved in loving relationships. Think about the extent to which you understood the connection between sexual relationships and pregnancy, the use of contraception and how awareness of the pregnancy occurred. Try to recall how news of the pregnancy was disclosed and what the immediate outcomes of that disclosure were.

81

Pregnancy and childbirth

While you describe the experience of being pregnant and the events that surrounded the pregnancy, think about issues of control and power and consider whether you felt a sense of disempowerment during this time. Think about motives and beliefs as well as expectations and priorities. It was often during this period that plans for the future were made. These plans were often made by others and your views and feelings may not have been considered. Try to remember when the adoption decision was made and whose interests it was expected to serve. In terms of the adoption decision, some mothers have seen themselves as the victim and some as the perpetrator. The truth is usually much more complex.

In the past, the difference between being married and being unmarried was very significant. Unmarried, pregnant women were often treated very differently in maternity hospitals from married, pregnant women. Many maternity hospitals did not allow unmarried expectant mothers to attend ante-natal classes and so they were unable to prepare for childbirth in the same way that married women did. In many hospitals there were rules which favoured married women and unmarried mothers were not allowed visitors or not allowed to have access to their newborn babies. It can be useful to recall the hospital experience and to consider how it felt to be subjected to such discriminatory policies.

Description of the birth itself can be traumatic for many mothers, especially for those who have never been invited to describe it before. Many mothers are unable to describe the experience of giving birth, however, either because they were not conscious during the event or because they have since lost the memory of it. For many mothers the outcome of the trauma experienced at that time has been loss of memory. For some there are moments which are clear and others which are completely lost to them.

It is often difficult for mothers to recall events which occurred shortly after the birth of their child. Most report a feeling of numbness and a sense of emotional distance from what was happening. Some can recall nothing for some time after the birth. Many mothers recall the behaviour and attitudes of medical personnel and other professionals, however, including issues around whether or not they were able to see or hold their babies. Reliving those experiences can cause buried rage to resurface.

Accessing relevant documents can be an important element of personal recovery work for mothers. Receiving a copy of your child's birth certificate, for example, validates your experience and your relationship to your child. Hospital and social work records may also be useful. Any other documents relevant to the adoption, which can be obtained, may assist in the exploration of the events. It is wise to bear in mind, however, that obtaining those documents can itself be a challenging experience and may resurrect a range of buried emotions. It may be wise to have a support person with you when accessing such documents.

Be aware also that the loss of your child may have been complicated by other, related losses. Many women lost the relationship which they had shared with the father of their child. For some, they had to leave employment or study or even move to a different area. Many lost friendships and close relationships within their families. For most mothers the adoption had an irreversible impact on their relationships with their parents. Reliving the loss of your child may bring to the surface connected losses which have also not been adequately grieved.

What has happened since

In many cases, making the decision that their child was to be adopted was presented to unmarried parents as the responsible course of action and was frequently described as 'doing the right thing'. On the other hand, it could be considered that, by being pressured into not raising the children whom they had created, those parents were actually being encouraged to avoid taking responsibility for the logical consequences of their behaviour. It is interesting to consider how they may have internalised that and the impact which that may have had on their behaviour later in life. It seems that some parents learned that not taking responsibility was acceptable behaviour and therefore acquired the habit of blaming others. Some, however, felt that they had shirked their responsibility to their children and took it upon themselves thereafter to be very responsible. They sometimes blamed themselves, throughout their lives, for anything that did not turn out well. This may have created a degree of tension in people's lives, which can have a negative impact on their general health.

Many original parents were afraid to succeed in their lives, after the loss of their children, as it may have appeared to others that they had gained from not raising their children. This put them in a no-win situation. If they did well in life, then they felt guilty. If they did not succeed in life, however, that allowed others to suppose that their child was indeed better off without them. The result can be that they become resentful and angry when people tell them that they seem to have 'done well', because this suggests that they had not suffered as a result of the separation from their child.

Part of the recovery process is sorting out the difference between facts and beliefs. It was a fact that the woman was pregnant. It was a belief held by some that she could not provide the best care for her child. It was a fact that she had had some kind of sexual relationship which had resulted in the pregnancy. It was a belief held by some that she was by virtue of that an immoral person and an unfit mother. While some facts are indisputable, beliefs can be challenged and they change over time. We each give our own meanings to the events of our lives.

Part of the recovery process is making links and connections and being able finally to understand what has been

84

happening in one's life. For example, a mother might have found that throughout her life she has had an aversion to signing her name and that completing forms of any kind is difficult for her. When it is pointed out to her that the first time she signed her name, as an adult, on a 'form' was to sign an adoption consent for her child, then her aversion is explained.

Some mothers have great difficulty remembering dates. When they realise that they had blocked out the date of the birth of their lost child, then they understand that having 'forgotten' that very important date, they would have felt guilty allowing themselves to remember other significant dates. Some mothers who lost their first child to adoption chose not to have any further children, as they felt that it would be disrespectful to that child.

Some mothers have had difficulty enjoying Mother's Day celebrations prior to reuniting with their child. They have, in many cases, sabotaged the attempts of the family to create an enjoyable day. When they realise that their guilt would not allow them to accept themselves as worthy of praise in their mothering role, then it becomes clear to them why they covertly made sure that they did not enjoy that day. Once they understand their own actions, they can make an effort to change their behaviour.

It is also helpful to examine the impact of the loss of the child on how you have dealt with subsequent significant events, especially losses. In many cases, where a significant loss had not been appropriately grieved, there was a very intense reaction to subsequent losses. In other cases, there appeared to be little reaction to subsequent losses, as a behaviour pattern of shutting down emotionally had been established at the time of the loss of the child.

Once you have a deeper understanding of your past, think about the strengths and strategies which you have already displayed, in order to be able to live with your experience and consider how you can put those strengths to use during the remainder of your life.

Summary

The aim of personal recovery work is to grieve the losses created by the adoption separation, by moving through the phases and tasks of mourning. Although it may not be possible for original parents or adopted adults to declare that issues have been addressed and will never recur, nevertheless it is possible to identify signs that mourners have been able to assimilate their loss and move on with life. Worden suggests that one sign that mourning is nearing completion is when we reach a stage in which times without pain can be enjoyed (Worden, 1991, p18). The pain may return but, over time, it erupts less frequently and less intensely. Personal recovery work on adoption separation issues can bring both adopted adults and their original parents to a point where they are able to enjoy life without feeling guilty.

When you have a sense that you have achieved a level of acceptance of the issues surrounding your adoption separation experience, it is likely that you will feel more comfortable sharing your experience with others. This can give you a sense of ownership of your experience and also contribute to community education and awareness. If you are able to present your experience to others in a powerful and confident manner, then you may find that you no longer feel any sense of shame.

For many, seeking reunion is a natural progression from the acknowledgement and exploration of the impact of adoption in their lives, which occurred during their personal recovery work. Those who have already achieved a degree of personal recovery prior to reunion are likely to bring more clarity and awareness, as well as less anger and sadness, to the reunion experience. For those who have not already acknowledged their grief, the experience of reunion itself can provide the impetus to embark on a programme of personal recovery work. Whether or not a reunion takes place, however, personal recovery work plays a vital role in the journey towards healing for those who have experienced an adoption separation.

4. Questions asked by adopted adults

Adopted people are really the innocent parties in this whole adoption business, as we had no say in what took place when we were born. Don't you agree that because of this we should have the right to make the decisions when it comes to search and reunion?

In my view it is unfortunate that people sometimes talk about adopted people as the 'innocent' parties to the adoption. This feeds into the notion that others (eg original mothers and fathers) were in some way the 'guilty' parties. I think it is more helpful to rid adoption of notions of guilt and blame altogether. What might your original parents have been 'guilty' of – of being young, of being vulnerable, of wanting the best that life could offer you? In fact none of us had control over what happened when we were born. No one chooses how or by whom they are going to be raised, whether they are adopted or not. Adopted adults make their own decisions about reunion, as do their original parents, but I do not believe that anyone has any superior right to decision-making.

I was recently reunited with my original mother. It's been a really difficult time for my adoptive mother, as she feels that my original mother is trying to replace her. Is there any way that I can help her to make the adjustment?

In some situations, people other than parents raise a child and act in a parental role. They may be grandparents, adoptive parents, foster parents, stepparents or anyone who cares for and raises a child, whether or not they have legal custody. The people who raise you, whether or not they are your parents, have a unique place in your life. When children become adults, their relationships with those who have had parental roles in their lives operate on a different level. When a reunion takes place between a mother and child who have been separated by adoption, the

87

mother will not replace the person who has acted in a maternal role in her absence. Each person has their place and their role in your life. For example, if your mother died and your father remarried, your stepmother would be an additional mother figure in your life. For some people, they have a mother who after a period of time is no longer there to care for them (whether through death, adoption or separation) and then there may be other maternal figures in their life. Your mother will always be your mother even if she is not physically present in your life. The same applies to fathers. Your father is your father whether he participates in your upbringing or not. There may be other people in your life who act in a paternal role and you may care deeply for them, but that does not change the facts. Hopefully your adoptive mother can come to understand that she has a unique place in your life, as does your original mother.

I've met both of my original parents and discovered that they were married a few years after I was adopted and have three more children who are my full siblings. They are still married and they seem to be such a happy family. I feel really cheated that I wasn't able to be a part of that family as I was growing up. I feel as if the other children were important enough to keep but I wasn't. Can I ever get over my anger with them for giving me away and then staying together?

The fact that your original parents are still together can be seen as an advantage, in one way, in that it means that you get to meet your father and mother together. It also shows you that you were born into a deep and loving relationship. I'm sure it's hard for them to confront the fact that you were raised separately from their other children, but the past cannot be undone. I hope that you can begin to find your place in your original family and enjoy the warmth that is there. Anger is common in reunion relationships and it's important that you find productive ways to

88

express it, without it preventing you from building a strong relationship with the members of your original family.

My original mother wants to meet me. I want to tell her that I'm quite happy and I already have a mother. How can I get that across to her without hurting her feelings?

    To be honest, I can't imagine how any mother could hear that kind of message and not be hurt by it. For many original mothers it is heartbreaking to discover that their child refuses to acknowledge their connection with their original families. I hope that you'll reconsider and find the courage and generosity to be able to offer your original mother a place in your life. Please give yourself some time to consider the situation more deeply.

I was adopted into a different country from the one I was born in and I would love to find my original family. However, I'm worried about how I can possibly build a relationship with family members if I do find them, as we won't speak the same language and my lifestyle has been very different from theirs. Do you think it would be better for me not to bother to try?

    Building a relationship with family members from whom one has been separated by adoption can be difficult for anyone, but in situations like yours, there are the added complications that you have mentioned. Part of your preparation for reunion could be learning some of your original language and learning about the lifestyle your original family members might have experienced. Many people who are adopted into other countries and cultures report the benefits of identifying with their original culture in addition to the culture in which they were raised.

My original mother wants me to visit her and sleep at her home. I tried that once before and it just made me feel really strange and emotional. I can't understand why, but I don't want to do it again. How can I tell her this without hurting her feelings?

Other adopted people have also told me that it affected them deeply to sleep under the same roof as their original mothers. Some have even felt that they wanted to sleep in the same bed with their mothers and this has scared them. Because of these feelings, some adopted people refuse invitations and then misunderstandings arise. I think it's all part of adjusting to the fact that your mother was not present during your childhood and so you are both struggling to establish a relationship for which there are no socially accepted norms. I think it would help if you are able to talk to your original mother about your feelings so that you are working on this issue together, instead of allowing it perhaps to turn into an area of conflict. Otherwise your mother may assume that you do not care about her and she may stop issuing invitations. Over time, I'm sure these feelings will gradually become less intense. Your relationship with your original mother does not have to meet any set standards. It belongs to you and her and it is up to both of you to build the kind of relationship which you both want to have.

I've been contacted by my original mother, but I feel that there are some issues that I want to sort out before I'm ready to meet her. I really want to know her, but I'm worried that she won't like me as I am and I want to take some time to make changes. Do you think she'll understand this and be able to wait until I'm ready?

I hope that your original mother will be able to be patient with you and allow you to move at your own pace. However, you don't have to be perfect before you're ready to meet her. It would be helpful for you to think about why you feel that you are not acceptable as you are. I hope that you have read some books about the impact of adoption and have had the opportunity to discuss adoption issues with someone who is familiar with the area. Hopefully your original mother will be able to accept you for who you are, her son, in the same way that you feel that you want to know her because she is your mother.

I've read a lot about the shame felt by mothers whose children were adopted. I have grown up being ashamed of being adopted. Is this common? I always felt that I was second-best, firstly because I was given away by my original parents and secondly because my adoptive parents couldn't have children of their own and so they had to settle for me. How can I get over my shame?

It's very sad that both sets of parents most likely thought that they were saving you from the disadvantages of illegitimacy, yet you have felt shame because you were adopted. Perhaps it would help if you try to take control over the information about your adoption, rather than allowing others to make you feel ashamed of it. You could find ways of explaining that you were adopted that feel positive and comfortable to you, such as saying, 'My mother was single when I was born and she didn't know where to go for help. The social worker convinced her that adoption was the best outcome for me', or 'My adoptive parents wanted to give a needy child the advantages of a family life'. Such explanations emphasise that the motivations which led to your adoption were positive and that the adoption happened because people cared about you and not because they didn't care about you. Being raised apart from your original families does not mean that you are inherently flawed in any way. Reunion helps people to own and accept their history so that the element of shame can be removed. It might be useful for you to learn about the experiences of parents who lost children through adoption, so that you can see how and why so many adoptions occurred. I don't believe it's helpful for original parents to feel guilty and ashamed for the fact that someone else raised their children. Nor do I think it's helpful for adoptive parents to be made to feel guilty or ashamed for having adopted. There's nothing inherently wrong with offering a home to a child who seems to need one. In most cases all the parents involved believed that they were acting in the best interests of the children. There is nothing wrong with wanting the best for your child. Adoption has obviously had a big impact

91

on your life, but it's still possible for you to reach a stage where you are comfortable with who you are. Talking to other people who were adopted and reading about their experiences can be useful, as can enlightened counselling.

I'm adopted and I had been thinking about searching for my original mother one day. However, she contacted me and took my choice away from me. I'm so angry that I had no choice when I was born and then I didn't have any choice about being contacted by my mother. Why couldn't she have left it up to me to make that decision?

Well, no one has any choice when they are born and it seems to me that your original mother has not taken anything from you. In fact, she has given you a great opportunity. All she did was let you know that she cares about you and that she is there for you, if you choose to meet her. You still have a choice. I hope that you can learn how to deal with your anger so that it will not interfere with the relationship between you and your mother. Many adopted people would be delighted if their original mothers made themselves available for reunion.

I was reunited with my original father recently and since our meeting he has showered me with gifts. He wants to take me on holidays and buy me a car. I appreciate his generosity, but it makes me feel uncomfortable, as it's almost as if he's either trying to buy my affection or else trying to make up with his money, for not being there for my mother when I was born. I don't know if he's kind to me because he cares about me or if he's just trying to ease his conscience. How can I explain this to him and ask him to back off a bit, without appearing rude or ungrateful?

Parents who have been reunited with their children often feel that they want in some way to 'make it up' to them. For some original parents, who have the financial means, one way to try to do that is to spend money on their children. I'm sure your father enjoys buying you gifts. He may see it as trying to make up for all the lost years, rather than trying to make amends for his behaviour. Hopefully, as you get to know each other better, you will feel more able to express your feelings honestly to him and be able to let him know that these extravagant gifts make you feel uncomfortable. It's unlikely that that is his intention. It would be better to be honest rather than withdraw and let him assume that you do not enjoy his company. Perhaps you could reassure him that you are happy to have him in your life and that time spent together is the most valuable gift he can offer.

I was very surprised when I was reunited with my original mother as I realised that some of the feelings I was having were similar to the feelings I had when my close friend died. On both occasions I felt numb and disbelieving, then overcome with sadness, then angry at what had happened. I'm wondering if there is any connection between adoption and death?

Many people describe similar feelings surrounding a death and an adoption reunion. In fact, being involved in an adoption reunion is like experiencing the death of the dream, or the death of the 'not-knowing'. The two experiences can certainly result in similar feelings and it's good to understand that, so that those involved can accept that how they feel is appropriate. Then they are able to move through those phases of grieving and hopefully come to a point where they are able to assimilate those loss experiences into their lives.

I read an article about post-reunion attraction and it really scared me. It seems that in a lot of adoption reunion situations, sexual relationships develop between family members. I'm thinking about searching for my original mother and I'd hate to find myself in a situation like that. Is there any way I can make sure that doesn't happen?

93

I've been involved with family members separated by adoption for many years. I've travelled extensively and have counselled many people who have been reunited with family members following an adoption separation. In all that time I have encountered only a very few situations in which family members had become sexually involved following an adoption reunion. While in many cases there is a feeling that reminds people of romantic attraction and while there is sometimes a desire for physical contact, actual sexual relationships in adoption reunion situations are rare. It's important to be aware, if you are hoping to have a reunion, that the feelings may be very intense, especially in the early stages of the reunion. If you prepare yourself for this, then hopefully you will be able to manage any feelings which arise. The vast majority of reunions do not result in inappropriate sexual relationships.

I've been reunited with my original mother and father (who are both married to other people) and now I find that my life is so complicated. My adoptive parents have divorced and have both remarried and so now I have four sets of 'parents' to accommodate and fit into my life. What should I call them all? What will my children call them? Is it possible to keep everybody happy? Who should take precedence?

Because so many relationships in our times do not last a lifetime, many people are dealing with complex family situations. Children are interacting with half-brothers and sisters as well as with people who might be known for example as 'my mother's boyfriend's daughter'. Children are able to work out who is related to whom and where everyone fits. Appropriate naming can be achieved by negotiation. No one automatically has precedence and it can be tricky to juggle the various family relationships with which we must deal, even where there has been no adoption in the family. However, we manage, because that is how life is.

94

My original mother tells me that she had 'no choice' but to give me up for adoption and that she 'didn't stand a chance' against her family, the social workers etc. I find it hard to believe her, as she seems to me to be a very strong and assertive woman. Sometimes I think that she's just trying to make up excuses. How can I know if she's being honest with me?

First of all, it would be helpful for you to try to gain some understanding of the situation your original mother was in at the time of her pregnancy. Her life experiences since that time and the way she has approached them may have allowed her to develop into a strong and assertive woman and for that I think she is to be applauded. However, at the time of your birth it is unlikely that she was able to assert her wishes. It might be helpful for you to read material written by those who experienced society's disapproval at that time, or talk to other people who found themselves in similar situations. That way you might learn about the factors which allowed some women to be mothers, while others became mothers who lost their children through adoption. Many societies have traditionally frowned upon mothers who sought to raise their children without fathers and often the mothers, rather than the fathers, have come to be blamed for such situations. Until Federal Government financial support for single parents was introduced in Australia in 1973, for example, it was almost impossible for a single woman, unaided, to provide financial support sufficient to raise a child alone. Even after government support became available, the social stigma and the resulting perceived disadvantage to the child deterred some mothers from attempting such a daunting task. Some mothers definitely did not have a choice. In some places, for example, if the mother was under age at the time of the pregnancy, her parents had the legal right to make a decision on her behalf. Some mothers were deceived and were not given accurate information which could have allowed them to make an informed choice. Some mothers feel that they did exercise a degree of choice, but that their options were so limited as to appear to be no option at all. Some believe that their consents were obtained under duress or while they were under the influence of hospital administered medication. Others believe that they thought the matter through and made the best choice possible under difficult circumstances. For almost all of the mothers I have ever encountered, who were separated from their children by adoption, there was considerable anguish related to the separation. I hope that you can come to understand and empathise with your mother and the many other mothers like her, who felt abandoned by society and pressured into parting with their children, because it was considered to be 'the right thing' to do.

It's been a year now since I was reunited with my original mother but sometimes I find that she is insensitive to my feelings and says hurtful things to me. Sometimes I just think I'd be better off not having her in my life. Why can't she be more understanding and think of my feelings more?

Without knowing exactly how your mother has hurt your feelings, it's hard to comment. Have you spoken to her about what it is that you find hurtful? It may be that your mother feels comfortable being honest with you. Only you can judge whether or not she is deliberately trying to upset you, or whether she is unknowingly causing you distress. I hope you can talk to her about this issue and come to some understanding rather than just run away from the relationship because you are finding aspects of it challenging. I'm sure that the relationship could be strengthened by some productive dialogue about areas which are painful for each of you. Hopefully you can discuss maturely how you can both be respectful of the other's feelings, without having to relate to each other in a constrained and uncomfortable manner.

I don't understand why, in 2009, adoptions are still taking place. I understand that a lot of people back in the 1960s and 1970s thought that adoption was the best outcome for illegitimate children. I've also read a lot of the research that has been conducted into the long term outcomes of adoption for adopted people and their original parents. We are now much more aware of the importance of genetic continuity and more respectful of the rights of children to be raised within their family and kinship groups. In this day and age, why haven't we worked out better ways to assist and support children at risk, than to sever their legal relationship to their entire families and issue them with false birth certificates?

I'm wondering that too.

I'm adopted and some people have suggested to me that I could try to find my original parents. I think it should be up to them to look for me and so I haven't done anything about it. I presume that they aren't interested, as I haven't heard anything from them. What do you think?

I think that you would be doing your original parents a great favour by letting them know that you are interested in them and would like to make contact. You can't assume just because you haven't heard from them that they would not like to know about you. They may not be able to get information about you. They may have been trying to find you but not succeeded. They may even have died. If you genuinely want to know your original parents, then I suggest that you do everything you can to locate them and then make them an offer of contact. Even if you are unable to find them immediately, you will have a sense of satisfaction from having tried and if you and your original parents do get in touch one day, they will know that you cared enough to try to contact them.

97

I really want to develop a relationship with my original mother, but sometimes I just don't know how to make conversation with her. I don't want to be always talking about adoption. Have you any suggestions?

Apart from the obvious one of finding out what things she's interested in and how she spends her time and asking her about those things, it's also good to find out which people are important in her life and ask after them too. If your mother has other children who are important to her, that may be hard for you to accept, but it will help if you show that you care about the people that she cares about. If she has a hobby or a lifestyle which makes you uncomfortable or simply bores you, that may be difficult for you too, but it will also help if you show that you are interested in what she does with her time and that you are prepared to accept her as she is and not expect her to change. As time goes on, hopefully it will get easier, as you get to know some of the people in her life, she gets to know some of the people in your life and you also get to share some experiences together. Hopefully she will make some effort too and enquire after the people and activities which are important to you.

I have been told that I was removed from my original parents under child protection legislation and adopted without their consent. This makes me wonder if they are horrible people and if I want to find them. I would really love to know more about my background but the circumstances of my adoption make the idea of searching for my original family very scary. What would you advise?

First of all, I would suggest that you apply to receive as much information about your adoption as you can, so that you will know the truth about the circumstances. There may have been misunderstandings at the time and also your parents have had many years to work on whatever issues may have been considered relevant at the time of your birth. Apart from your parents, there

98

may be other family members, siblings and grandparents for example, who were completely innocent in the matter of your care and who would be delighted to know you. I suggest that if you discover that you were indeed adopted without the consent of your parents, that you proceed cautiously, bearing in mind your own safety, but, at the same time, be open to the idea that there may well be a great deal for you to gain by discovering more about your past.

I was adopted and I also gave up my child for adoption. At the time it just seemed like the right thing to do, but now I'm really sad that adoption has affected yet another generation. Is it common for women who were adopted to lose their children through adoption? How can I sort out all the complicated relationships that have been created in my family?

It does happen quite often that women who have been adopted lose custody of their children in one way or another, sometimes through adoption and sometimes less formally. They may also be involved in arranging adoptions, thereby separating other parents from their children. As far as I am aware, there is no research to explain this. It seems that for some, they want somehow to reinforce the idea that adoption was a good thing in their lives and the way to do that is to create yet another adoption situation. Some women seem to think that it will help to reduce the shame and embarrassment they feel about having parents who chose not to raise them, if they then choose not to raise their children also, or support other parents to make this choice. Adopted people are said to lack genealogical continuity. For some women this means that because they have been raised in an adoptive situation, they have not been able to appreciate the significance of blood relationships. If they have not addressed their own issues in relation to this, they may believe that children are interchangeable and that it makes no difference to them in which families they are raised. For other women, they lack confidence in their ability to relate to their own child, because they have been raised among people to whom they are not related and they panic at the thought of taking on the responsibilities of parenthood. Whatever the reasons, it's a complex situation, but one that can be confronted and dealt with. Many people's lives are complex and approaching the situation with honesty and generosity will make it easier for everyone to manage.

I've searched and searched for my original mother but have been unable to find her. I know nothing about my original father. Will I have to spend the rest of my life in a state of constant anxiety wondering if I'll ever meet them or should I just forget the whole thing and get on with my life?

It's difficult to strike a balance between being aware of the desire to be reunited with your original parents, but also being realistic and accepting of the fact that it is not happening at the moment and, like other hopes and dreams, may never happen. It never ceases to amaze me how people do find each other and so I hope that you won't give up hope. However, if you can find a way to incorporate this into your life, then there is no need for your disappointment to prevent you from having a fulfilling life. It might be helpful to practise talking about it in a positive way. For example, if the topic of family comes up in conversation, you could say that you were adopted and that you have tried to locate your original families but so far have not been successful. That confirms that it is an important part of your life, but that you are realistic about the difficulties involved. You also never know who might have some useful suggestions for searching that you hadn't thought of before.

I'm adopted and I was raised in a family which had a different racial background from the one into which I was born. On the one hand it was obvious as I grew up that I was adopted and so there was no secrecy, but on the other hand, the obvious physical differences between my adoptive family and me made me feel isolated and alone. It has also made it very difficult for me to relate to the racial group into which I was born. Are there others like me who feel that they just don't fit anywhere?

There are many people like you who have been raised in a racial and cultural environment in which they have felt out of place and among people who did not reflect them in any way. It may be helpful for you to meet with others who have had similar experiences or to read books written by trans-racially adopted people. I hope that you will learn to assimilate your adoption experience into your life and acknowledge your true value, as an individual with a unique mix of cultural influences.

My adoptive parents didn't have good parenting skills and I suffered what I now recognise to be emotional abuse throughout my childhood. I ended up in foster care when I was thirteen. A few years later I was reunited with my original parents, who had married and had a happy life without me. They have no other children and are quite well-off. I feel really resentful that they have had such a good life and I had such a rotten life. How can they just expect me to welcome them back into my life when it looks as if I suffered so that they could enjoy life's luxuries?

I'm sure when your original parents allowed you to be adopted, they wanted what was best for you. There is no way they could have predicted the kind of life you have had. Do you know why it was that they had no other children? Anecdotal evidence suggests that approximately one third of parents who have been separated from a child through adoption have no further children. I can understand that you are angry, but have you looked closely at who was responsible for your suffering? I'm sure your original parents never wanted you to have a miserable life. Your adoptive parents, on the other hand, obviously lacked the skills and compassion needed for their role. It might be helpful for you to learn about the situation your original parents were in when they agreed to your adoption, as that may help you to see more clearly where the responsibility lies. The bottom line is that you are now an adult and responsible for your own choices. However, if your original parents care about you and are interested in you, then perhaps they could help you to overcome your early disadvantages and have a fulfilling life in spite of them, as many people have done.

I obtained my original birth certificate and after seeing it, I don't think I want to find my original parents. There was virtually nothing on it. My original mother didn't even give me a name and under 'father' it just says 'not named'. I suppose that means that either she didn't know who had got her pregnant or else he wasn't interested enough to put his name down. Why would I want to meet these people who obviously didn't care anything about me when I was born?

Many mothers who lost children to adoption were not allowed to name their children. Many fathers were not allowed to be recognised as fathers, simply because they were not married to the child's mother. It's unwise to make assumptions from such a document. My experience shows that original birth certificates do not represent how the parents felt at all, but instead often represent how they were excluded from the process and their experiences and their relationship to their child were discounted. I hope that you will be able to contact your original parents and hear from them how they really felt. In some places names can be added later to the original birth certificate.

I received a letter from a social worker saying that my original mother wants to hear from me. I refused any contact because I don't feel that there's anything missing in my life and I don't feel any need to be in touch with my original mother. Do you think that means that there's something wrong with me?

Some people would find your response rather odd. If I called you and invited you to a show, for example, would you tell me that you wouldn't go because you don't feel any need to go to a show? If someone invites you somewhere or offers you the opportunity to go somewhere or meet someone, I'm sure it's not because they think that you are somehow lacking because you have not had that experience. Accepting an invitation does not imply that you were already feeling that something was missing. Invitations and opportunities are made available to us so that we can choose to enrich our lives and add to our experiences. That doesn't suggest that our lives were not rich before. I don't think you have to feel that something is missing in your life before you can accept an invitation to meet someone. Of course, an invitation to an adoption reunion is much more significant than other invitations in life and so I hope that you'll give it more consideration before you reach a decision. Rather than thinking in terms of what might or might not be missing from your life, maybe you could focus instead on the opportunity that's being offered. Many people in your situation would be overjoyed to receive such a letter.

My original mother got in touch with me and I discovered that she had been searching for me for some time. While I appreciate that she was interested in me, when I found out that she had obtained copies of my school photographs and had found out about the births of my children, I felt really invaded. Don't you agree that it's not right for someone to obtain personal information like that about someone they've never even met?

Parents who have been separated from their children by adoption are usually cut off from any knowledge or information about those children and often are desperate to know if their child is still alive, is in good health, has been well-cared for and generally what has become of them. There is no legal barrier to obtaining publicly available information and, for many original

103

parents, finding out about their children's lives in this way is their only option to having to live with the agony of never knowing, wondering and worrying. You are right that this effort your mother has made does indicate how much she cares about you and is interested in you. Your original mother is not someone whom you have 'never even met'. You were intimately connected for nine months and shared the unique experience of your birth. I hope that you can try to understand what the separation might have meant to her and remember that her actions were well-intentioned. Hopefully you and your original mother can go on to build a close relationship and can learn from each other about the time spent apart.

I've been reunited with my original parents but they seem to have a hard time accepting me for who I am. My lifestyle is quite different from theirs and I seem to be such a disappointment to them. Why can't they just accept me as I am?

It's very sad that your original parents seem to you to be so judgmental and seem to be focussing on your lifestyle rather than the fact that you are their son. Are you able to discuss your feelings with them? Perhaps they don't realise that you sense disappointment in them. It may be that they are not disappointed in you as a person, but that meeting you has forced them to face the fact that they lost the opportunity to raise you. Parents often wonder how their children's lives might have been different, if the adoption had not taken place. Perhaps you can reassure them that you are happy in your lifestyle and then they might be better able to focus on the positive aspects of your relationship with them.

I have good relationships with both my adoptive parents and my original parents but I find that other people just don't understand. They don't seem to realise how important it is to adopted people to know about their heritage. How can I help them to understand?

104

The more adoption is brought out into the open and talked about as a part of life, the better others will understand the issues. I know some people are very narrow-minded and just don't want to hear. In cases like that, perhaps you could say something like, 'I'm sorry that you don't seem to understand how I feel. I can appreciate that it must be difficult for you, as you weren't adopted like me. I'd be happy to try to help you to understand.'

I contacted my original mother and we spoke once on the telephone. I would really love to exchange letters with her and some day to meet her, but she says that her husband (who is not my father) will not 'allow' her to have any more contact with me. I can't understand how a mature woman could allow her husband to dictate to her in that way. Do you have any suggestions for me?

Sadly, many mothers were bullied into giving up their children and, as a result, submitting to bullying became a habit for them. Some original mothers have been able to understand what happened to them and have used their experience to make sure that they are no longer submissive and compliant, as they may have been when they lost their children. Others, however, have not gained strength from their loss, but rather have gone through their lives as victims. I would suggest that you tell your original mother that you care about her and will continue to contact her regularly, but perhaps not frequently for now. Hopefully your messages will finally lead her to gain the confidence and courage she needs, to refuse to tolerate her husband's bullying and to accept your generous offer of reunion.

My mother died when I was ten years old. My father later remarried and I was adopted by my stepmother. They eventually divorced but then I was horrified, when I was planning my marriage, to be told that my original birth certificate with my mother's name on it was no longer a legal document and that I would have to record my stepmother's name as my mother. I

105

knew and loved my mother and I haven't seen my stepmother for years. I had no idea that being adopted by her would mean that for the rest of my life I would have to deny my own mother. Can I have the adoption reversed?

In most places it's not legally possible to have an adoption rescinded, but I suggest that you seek legal advice in the area in which you were adopted. It may also be useful to you to seek counselling around your adoption situation.

Although I've always known that I was adopted, I was never interested in trying to find my original relatives. In fact, I had no idea that I even had another birth certificate until recently. Then I made enquiries and was able to obtain a copy of my original birth certificate, which had my original name on it and my original mother's name. I was just amazed at how deeply that affected me. I was suddenly confronted with the reality that I existed as a person before my adoption. I felt as if the rug had been pulled from under me. I've been really emotional ever since, but now I just feel paralysed and don't know what to do next. What would you advise?

I don't believe that having your birth certificate has caused you to be upset, but rather that it has triggered the emotions which have been buried deeply inside, since you were separated from your families of origin. Many adopted people say that their adoption had never been an issue for them, when what they mean is, that they had buried their feelings and chosen not to explore its implications in their lives. I think that the first thing is for you to accept your feelings and understand that they are appropriate. Once you feel that you have begun to accommodate your grief, then you may have the confidence to proceed, knowing that you will benefit from knowing the truth, no matter what the outcome. It's important that you go at your own pace and be prepared to accept whatever you find with equanimity. You're on an exciting journey, unlike anything you have ever experienced.

Whatever happens, it will be a tremendous growing and learning experience for you.

I was reunited with my original mother recently and we get on well, but I wish she would stop trying to act like a 'mother' to me! I already have one mother who nags me and that's enough. How can I explain this to her without hurting her feelings?

Well, she is one of your mothers, but when we become adults we work out how our relationships with our parents are going to be managed. Each relationship is unique. Of course, the relationship between a parent and an adult child whom they have not raised has additional dimensions. All parents respond differently to their children becoming adults and some manage the transition better than others. It sounds as if your original mother cares about you and wants to be helpful. I'm sure you can find a sensitive way to acknowledge her intentions, but let her know what it is about her behaviour that makes you uncomfortable. Over time, hopefully, you will be able to work co-operatively and create a relationship that suits both of you.

I can't understand why so many mothers just gave away their babies in the 1960s and 1970s. How could they have done that?

In those days there was a lot of shame and guilt attached to an out-of-wedlock pregnancy. Reputation was very important then. Young women were often judged on the basis of their sexual reputations and the whole family could be stigmatised on the basis of the behaviour of one member. In many cases, the parents of the mother could not tolerate an illegitimate grandchild, as this was considered by many to bring shame on the whole family. Illegitimate children also carried the shame and guilt from their parents and were sometimes considered inferior. At one time, for example, anyone who was illegitimate was barred from entering university (this actually happened to Leonardo Da Vinci). In the past, illegitimate children could not inherit from their mothers,

107

never mind their fathers, because an illegitimate child was considered to be 'the child of no one'. Parents were told that allowing their child to grow up illegitimate would constitute a very real disadvantage for the child. Also many mothers were not supported by the fathers of their children and if they also did not have support from their parents, they had no way of providing financially either for themselves or for a child. There were no government benefits then which would have supported single parent families as single parenthood was considered undesirable and therefore to be discouraged, not encouraged. Without family support, it was virtually impossible for single mothers to work. Without childcare, they couldn't undertake employment. Without employment, they would be unable to pay for accommodation. It's very interesting that after a federal government payment was created for single mothers in Australia in 1973, the number of adoptions reduced dramatically. This suggests that, for many mothers, lack of financial support was a major factor. Mothers were frequently told that it would be selfish of them to try to raise their children if they were not married and that they should put their children's welfare first and give them the opportunities in life that a married couple could provide. It might be helpful for you to read some of the work produced by original mothers and fathers, describing their experiences. With hindsight, many of them feel that their vulnerability was exploited.

I'm adopted and my original father has sent me a letter. I didn't think he had the right to do that. Does he?

As far as I know there is no law that prevents a person from writing a letter to another person. I assume that his letter is not threatening or abusive in any way. If your original father has written to you, then that suggests that he cares about you and is interested in you. As far as I'm aware, it's neither illegal nor morally wrong to care enough to write someone a letter. I hope that you'll appreciate his effort and consider responding positively to him. There are many adopted people who would be delighted to receive such a letter.

It's been wonderful to meet my original mother again, but it seems to me that for her, meeting me brings back all her hurt and sadness from the time I was born. I feel guilty that I was the cause of such pain. It's hard to enjoy being with her when I can see the hurt in her eyes, especially if I talk about my childhood or my adoptive family. Will she ever get over this and be able to enjoy spending time with me?

Your original mother is working through her grief, but she may benefit from some assistance. Perhaps you could suggest to her that she find a way to explore her grief and work through it in a way that will not impinge on her relationship with you. It seems to be difficult for her to hear about the life which you led without her. Perhaps she is not quite ready for that yet.

I never quite felt that I belonged in my adoptive family and always felt like the cuckoo in the nest. I searched for my original families in the hope of obtaining that sense of belonging, but I didn't feel it there either. Now I'm angry that I'm left to feel like a permanent outsider in society. How can I learn to live with that?

You are connected to your adoptive family socially and to your original families biologically but it seems that neither of those connections has given you the sense of total belonging that you seek. You can never be connected biologically to your adoptive family but it is possible to build social connections in your families of origin. If that doesn't happen, then I suggest that you focus on your sense of self-worth and how you can increase that independently of your family relationships and perhaps acknowledge the contributions that all of your family connections have made to the person that you have become.

I was so determined to belong to my adoptive family that I absorbed everything about the family and made it mine. I believed that I saw resemblances to members of my adoptive family and when I went to the doctor I confidently described my adoptive family's medical history as my own. Then I met the family of my original mother and discovered that not only do I look like all of them, but I also have inherited some medical issues from them. Now I feel such a fool for deceiving myself for all those years. How can I rewrite my history in an honest way and let go of those years of denial?

I believe that a programme of re-grief therapy would be very useful to you, in which you can recreate your life story from an honest perspective. This would help you to acknowledge openly the various contributions from both families and replace your fantasy story with a factual one. You may wish to do this by yourself or find a professional who is aware of the issues.

I met my original mother but afterwards I wished that I hadn't. She takes drugs, she has no job and she just seems to have drifted through life and not achieved anything. It just seemed that we have nothing at all in common. So after meeting her once I told her that I wasn't interested in seeing her again. I was so disappointed and so I just felt that there was no point. She's upset and says I should never have searched for her if I was just going to disappear out of her life again. Do you think she's right?

It's not uncommon for family members who have been separated by adoption to find that they have taken quite different journeys through life and that they do not share the same values. However this also happens in families where there has been no adoption separation experience. Your original mother is your mother regardless of the circumstances which she has had to face in her life and the ways in which she has chosen to deal with those circumstances. Your mother is not responsible for your disappointment. If you had certain expectations of her, which she

110

has not met, then you are the one who is responsible for your disappointment, not your original mother. No one can predict what they will experience after a reunion has occurred. I hope that you will think about this a bit more and find a way to accept your differences and be able to acknowledge your relationship.

I'm adopted and since being reunited with my original parents, I always seem to feel that it's my job to keep everyone happy. I frantically try to juggle time spent with both sets of parents so that I don't upset any of them. Will it always be this difficult?

Many adopted people seem to feel responsible for the feelings of others. Perhaps it would be helpful to you to read about the impact of adoption on the lives of those who are adopted and that might help you to understand better why you feel the way you do. You are not responsible for the feelings of others. All of your parents are adults and they are responsible for their own feelings. They all have to learn to deal with the impact of adoption on their lives. I suggest that you just relax and enjoy your time with them.

When I was reunited with my original mother, I told her that I had had a good upbringing and that I was grateful for having been adopted. Isn't that what original mothers want to hear?

Many original parents find it hurtful to hear adopted people say that they are 'glad' that they were adopted or that they are 'grateful' for having been adopted. It often translates to parents as, 'I'm so glad I wasn't raised by you – how awful would that have been?' I sometimes hear adopted people say that if they hadn't been adopted they would have had a poor and unhappy childhood. No one knows that. No one can ever know what might have happened. They may not have been poor – and besides, being poor does not necessarily mean being unhappy, any more than being rich guarantees happiness. Many poor people have a very rich emotional life, while many rich people are miserable.

111

Being young and poor is not a permanent condition and having a young, poor parent is also not necessarily a harmful environment for children. There are much worse situations.

My original mother says that she never actually had sexual intercourse with my father. Surely she must be wrong?

I've heard of cases where a pregnancy has resulted from sexual behaviour which apparently stopped short of actual intercourse. It's certainly possible and, in the social climate in which your original parents were growing up, not unheard of at all. For previous generations, the attitude to sexual behaviour before marriage was not open and accepting as it is in many societies now. Young people were expected to refrain from sexual intercourse until they were married and that is why there was such a degree of shame attached to an out-of-wedlock pregnancy. Such sexual behaviour as did occur was generally rather frantic and furtive. You have to remember also that, at that time, there was no sex education in schools and that most young people were very naïve when it came to the mechanics of sexual intercourse. Contraceptives were not readily available, nor was information. In many cases there was uncertainty about whether or not actual intercourse had occurred and, for many young women, who did not believe that they had participated in a completed act of intercourse, the pregnancy came as an enormous shock.

I was always quite content with the fact that I was adopted. I felt that I accepted it and didn't let it affect me very much. I was never interested in looking for my original parents, but then I got a telephone call from my original father. When I realised who it was, I burst into tears and cried for days afterwards. I couldn't decide if I was happy or sad. Why do you think it affected me that way?

I think that you actually had deep feelings of grief created by the separation from your parents, although it seems that you

112

did not recognise those feelings until your father's call triggered them. It sounds as if his contact brought to the surface a sense of loss and sadness for you that you had buried without being aware of it. I'm delighted for you that your father has contacted you and that you have been given the opportunity to acknowledge your grief. I hope that you will go on to explore and express your feelings, as you build relationships with your original relatives.

Why do some original mothers and fathers object to being called 'birthparents' (or 'birth parents')?

Many people are concerned about the use of terms such as these. Some parents feel that if they are referred to as the 'birthparents' (or 'birth parents') then that suggests that they are not actual parents, but only the parents who caused the birth to happen. For some, it implies that they were simply 'breeders'. Using that term can seem to suggest that after the birth they were no longer parents. Many original parents find the term insulting and demeaning. I know that there are some, however, who do not. The key point is that you discuss with your original parents how they prefer to be named and that you are able to reach an agreement on the matter.

When I was 45 I received a letter from a lawyer telling me that my father had died. I thought they must have made a mistake and told them that my mother was dead but my father was still alive. The lawyer informed me that my original father had died. My parents divorced when I was very young, my mother remarried and I was adopted by my stepfather. I was shocked. I discovered that my original father had been searching for me for many years and that I was his only child. I feel very angry that I was deceived all my life, but I'm glad that I did find out the truth, as it helped to explain a lot of things for me. How could anyone have thought that it was morally acceptable to lie to me all those years?

113

It's difficult to apply the views of today to the decisions made in the past. Some parents thought that they should try to protect their children from the pain that the knowledge of their adoption might bring. Others did not want to face the truth for reasons of their own. I hope that you can work through your outrage and disappointment and consider the positive experiences which you have had in your life and how you have made the most of your opportunities. Hopefully you can find some of your original father's relatives and find out about him from them.

I've read some horror stories about unmarried mothers being mistreated and having their babies taken from them illegally. How could society have allowed that to happen?

Some mothers certainly were treated very badly. This was partly because they were considered by some to be deserving of punishment, because they had committed the 'sin' of being single and pregnant. Also, those who strongly supported adoption for children of unmarried mothers were sometimes afraid that mothers would become attached to their babies and then manage to avoid adoption and so they employed various harsh tactics to ensure that the adoptions would go ahead. This usually occurred in situations where the mother had no one to protect her and fight for her rights.

It's not my fault I was adopted. My original parents abandoned me when I was a baby and gave me up for adoption. How can I ever forgive them for that?

I don't think it's helpful to talk about adoption in terms of fault. Were your original parents at fault for wanting you to have the advantages they thought they couldn't give you? Were your adoptive parents at fault for wanting to give a child a home and family? Was society at fault for not supporting family preservation and instead removing children from their families? I really don't think that trying to apportion blame is going to be

114

helpful. In my experience it often creates bitterness. Personally, I don't use the word 'forgive' as it has connotations of sin and guilt, which I don't find useful. Every parent I have ever met, who has lost a child through adoption, had been told that their child would benefit from being adopted. It is difficult to understand, therefore, how some adopted people consider that allowing them to be adopted was some kind of 'sin' on the part of the parents, for which the adopted adult may or may not choose to forgive them. Cases in which children were truly 'abandoned' are very rare. For most original parents they had no notion of abandoning their children at all. If the adopted adult feels that they did not, in fact, benefit in any way from being adopted, then it seems unfair to hold their original parents responsible. If the adoptive parents did not provide the child with a supportive and fulfilling home atmosphere in which to grow up, then whose responsibility is that? People act in line with their beliefs. Many unmarried parents were led to believe that there were circumstances in their lives which would be detrimental to their children's growth and development and that adoptive parents would not find themselves in such circumstances. Parents who were unmarried were also told that their children would suffer from the stigma of being labelled as illegitimate. Do you really think it's about forgiving?

I've been reunited with my original mother and I've discovered that she has very little education and has spent her life working in unskilled jobs. I was raised in a family which places a high value on education and all the members of my adoptive family have professional qualifications. I find it difficult to communicate with my mother because of her low level of education. Do you have any suggestions?

It might help to foster the relationship if you are able to emphasise the similarities between you and your original mother and not place too much stress on the differences. Your original mother does not have to earn her place in your life, no matter

115

what path her life has taken. Hopefully you can reassure her that your feelings for her are not dependent on her achievements, but that you care for her because you are her daughter. Perhaps she has admirable qualities which are not taught in institutions of higher learning. If you are able to approach the relationship with sensitivity and compassion, then I'm sure that the differences between you do not need to have a negative impact on your future together.

I'm adopted and I'm confused about who my 'relatives' are. Are they members of my adoptive family or members of my original families or all of them?

Adoption creates a close legal relationship and sometimes this results in a close emotional relationship. Sometimes it does not. A husband and wife have a legal relationship, for example, but they do not share the same genes. Having a blood relationship does not necessarily create an emotional closeness, any more than having a legal relationship does. However, there is a distinction between those to whom we are related by blood and those to whom we are related by a legal connection such as marriage or adoption. However, it's up to you to choose who you want to consider your relatives.

A woman came to my door claiming to be my mother. She's the woman who gave birth to me, but as far as I'm concerned that doesn't make her my mother. I've had a very happy upbringing and am quite content with my life as it is. I have a mother and I'm not looking for another one. How dare this woman intrude in my life like that? How can I make sure that I never hear from her again?

In my view, the woman who gave birth to you is your original mother, but I understand that, since you have no memory of her and no experience of a relationship with her, it may be difficult for you to think of her in those terms. This woman,

116

however, does have a memory of you and certainly has experienced a relationship of sorts with you, having carried you and given birth to you. Clearly she feels that she is your mother, by virtue of those memories and that experience which she shared with you. It seems that she has taken you by surprise and approached you when you did not feel ready for reunion. Hostility is sometimes present in reunion experiences, especially in situations where one of the parties has not prepared themselves for a reunion. Perhaps now that your original mother has come back into your life, you could consider your options more carefully. You could perhaps appreciate the opportunity which she has given you and use the occasion to think about exploring the impact of adoption on your life.

I read books about mothers who gave up their children for adoption and felt that I had some understanding of what it might have been like for my original mother to have given me up. However, when I eventually met her, she was very cool about it all and said that the pregnancy had come at an inconvenient time, when she wanted to pursue her career. She doesn't seem to have suffered much from having been separated from me, which is quite disappointing. Is it just not such a big deal for some original mothers?

It's impossible to generalise about adoption outcomes, as there are so many variables. I believe that most original parents suffer deeply from the loss of their children, but I have met some who seem to have been able to process their feelings at the time of the loss and so, in later years, perhaps at the time of reunion, they seem to be less affected emotionally. There are others, however, who have been very successful at shutting down their emotions and denying their feelings. For those original mothers, even when a reunion takes place, they are still not willing to get in touch with their buried feelings, because they fear being overwhelmed by the pain. I cannot guess what might be happening for your original

117

mother, but I do know that I have never met a mother who lost a child through adoption who was not deeply affected by the separation.

My original mother refuses to tell me who my father is. My original father and his family are my relatives too and I want to know about them. Is there anything I can do if my mother refuses to help me?

It's very sad that your original mother has chosen not to support you in seeking your father. Hopefully she will come to realise that you are a product of two parents and that it is in your best interests to have knowledge and understanding about both of your families of origin. It may be that your original mother has not addressed her own issues regarding her relationship with your father. If she continues to refuse to assist you, there may be documents relating to the adoption which might provide you with information, or there may be other family members who know of your original father. I hope you won't give up, as there are many potential benefits, for all three of you (you, your mother and your father) in confronting the events of the past and in exploring possible relationships for the future. Perhaps you could try to talk to your mother about this again and hope that she will come to see these benefits.

My original mother and I have been reunited but we don't feel like mother and daughter. I don't think of her as my mother and we feel more like friends. Is that normal?

You are mother and daughter, regardless of whether or not you 'feel like' mother and daughter. There is no set pattern for how a mother and daughter feel about each other. Some mothers and daughters hate each other and some mothers and daughters love each other. How you feel about each other doesn't have to be compared with how other people feel about each other. What you are (ie mother and child, or brother and sister) is a separate issue from how you feel. Once you openly acknowledge how you are connected, then you can begin to consider your relationship. It's your relationship and it's up to both of you to shape it. Denying the relationship, however, is not productive. If you are an adopted person and you meet the woman who gave birth to you, you have not met a friend, you have met your original mother. If your mother died in childbirth and you never knew her or if you are separated from her shortly after your birth and you grow up not knowing her, that does not alter her relationship to you. Some people have close relationships with their mothers; some do not. Some people have no interaction with their mothers at all. Acknowledging who our family members are, however, is an important factor in defining who we are and where we fit in the world.

I'm adopted. That means that my original parents rejected me when I was born. Why should I let them into my life now? What if they reject me again?

When your original parents gave up the right to raise you, it was not because of any individual traits or qualities that you possessed. They probably knew little, if anything, about you. They may not even have seen you. Because they had to make a decision about the implications of the family and social situation in which they found themselves and to try to predict how it would affect both you and them, that doesn't mean that they rejected you. It was not a personal decision, in that they did not regard you personally as in any way an undesirable child. You may have felt rejected but that is a feeling, not a fact. I have never yet heard a mother or father say that in allowing their child to be adopted, they were rejecting or abandoning that child. Such terminology can be very hurtful to original parents. For those adopted people who believe that, as a baby, they were somehow not good enough for their parents and were therefore given away, it can be helpful to look at themselves as they are and to realise that their original

119

parents had no way of knowing what that baby would become. If your original parents now refuse contact with you, that doesn't mean that they will be rejecting you either. It could mean that they are not willing to confront the truth and deal with their grief issues at this time in their lives. If they know nothing about you, they can't reject you personally. It may feel like a rejection, but, in fact, it would be a refusal on their behalf to face the truth and the implications of the past. Adopted people who are considering reunion may want to think about what there is about what they have become, that their original parents may appreciate and enjoy. Making contact with your parents is a risk, of course. It takes courage. You have no way of knowing whether or not they are ready for such a contact, but hopefully you will be able to overcome your fear and offer them that opportunity.

I'm so amazed at how much my health has improved since I was reunited with my original parents. I used to suffer from a variety of health issues, some of which the medical profession could not explain. Now I feel so much better. I know some adopted people say that they search to get medical information, but have you heard of people whose health has improved after reunion even without receiving any medical information?

Yes, I certainly have. For many adopted people and their original parents, the separation and the reactions to the loss have caused a range of health problems. The stress related to burying the grief has also been a factor. In many cases, being able to confront the reality of the separation and grieve the loss brings relief from those problems and a noticeable improvement in overall well-being.

I've been thinking about trying to trace my origins but I want to make it clear that I'm not looking for a mother, as I already have a mother. I would really just like some medical information from the woman who gave birth to me. I think she owes it to me to provide that. Don't you agree?

First of all, if you find the woman who gave birth to you, you will have found your original mother. You will have found a living, breathing, feeling person, not just a provider of information. In fact, your original mother does not owe you anything. I think it would be wise for you to try to prepare yourself a bit more for the implications of searching for your original mother, before you go any further with your plans and to remember that no one can predict what they will experience after the reunion has occurred.

I've often wondered about the families from which I came, but my adoptive parents have been so good to me. Do you think it would be disloyal to them if I try to contact my original parents?

Many adoptive parents are delighted when their adopted children try to find out about their original families, as they see it as a sign that they have raised them to accept themselves as being made up of a combination of their heritage and their environment. Getting in touch with your original identity can be a great opportunity for growth and personal fulfilment for all concerned.

I met up with my original mother a few years ago and it was a great reunion, but after a couple of years the relationship just seemed to die a natural death. It seems that her curiosity has been satisfied and that she has lost interest in me. Should I just leave things as they are?

Many people come and go in our lives. Some people enter our lives and remain there until one of us dies; other people are in our lives for a period of time and then we drift apart. A relationship usually will only continue to thrive if both parties want the relationship enough to put some effort into it. Sometimes misunderstandings arise and assumptions are made. Your mother may also be dealing with other issues in her life at this time, of which you are unaware. It might be a good idea to let your original mother know that you still care for her and that you are still willing to maintain some kind of contact, even if it's only an occasional card, letter or e-mail. It wouldn't take much effort and she may be delighted to know that you still care. On the other hand, if she has no interest in maintaining a relationship, at least you might find that out and can stop wondering.

I've thought about trying to find my original parents, but I've heard that most adoption reunions don't work out and I'm afraid of being hurt. Should I take the risk or just let sleeping dogs lie?

I have never understood why people talk about adoption reunions in terms of whether or not they 'work out'. When someone is raised within the family to which they were born, I never hear them say that their relationships with family members 'didn't work out', in spite of the fact that, when they are adults, they have good relationships with some family members but not with others. If a mother and child do not have a close relationship, regardless of whether or not they have spent the child's developing years together, does that mean that that particular mother/child relationship did not 'work out'? Or does it mean that mother/child relationships, in general, do not 'work out'? Some mothers and their adult children have close relationships and some do not. Many adopted adults have close relationships in both their families of origin and their adoptive families. They do not necessarily have equally close relationships with all family members, any more than do adults who are raised in their families of origin. Of course, seeking out your families of origin is a step into the unknown and takes courage. Sometimes fear overrides generosity of spirit and holds a person back from reaching out and meeting a family member from whom they have been separated by adoption. When people understand what it is that is happening to them, they will already be less fearful.

I would really like my original parents and my adoptive parents to get on well together as they are all important to me. They have never met, but my birthday is coming up and I was thinking about inviting all of them so that they could meet. I just want to be part of one big, happy family. Do you think this is a good idea?

First of all, for adopted people (and their various parents) their birthday is often an occasion of mixed emotions and so your birthday party is probably not a good choice for this sort of meeting. While you may want your original parents and your adoptive parents to like each other, this may not happen. I think it would be better if you leave it up to them to decide if and when they want to meet. Perhaps you could just emphasise to them how important they are to you and let them decide if and when they want to share time together.

I've thought about trying to find my original parents, but some people are telling me that it would be selfish of me to contact them, as I would be invading their privacy. I don't want to ruin their lives by bringing up the past for them. Do I have the right to do that?

A mother who has lost a child through adoption knows that she has had a child. Many fathers who have lost children through adoption also know that they have fathered a child. All of these mothers and fathers know that there is a possibility that there will be a reunion with that child one day. Some have chosen to anticipate and prepare themselves for the possibility of that event and some have not. There are, of course, cases where the original parents were led to believe that the child had died and there are fathers who were never told about the pregnancy. These parents have had no opportunity to prepare themselves. You have no way of knowing how ready your original parents might be to meet you again, but you will be doing them a great favour by giving them that opportunity. In my view, it's not about rights, it's about opportunities. I don't think that making contact with your original parents would be selfish. In fact I believe it is a very generous act.

I was so happy to find my original mother and father. They are both really nice people and I get on well with them. My adoptive parents are also very nice people and I had a really happy childhood. I've read a lot about the loss and grief associated with adoption, but I just don't seem to feel that way. Am I missing something?

Well, every loss situation is unique and everyone responds to loss in their own way. For some people their sense of loss after an adoption separation is less intense than it is for others. I wouldn't go looking for pain, if it doesn't seem to be there. Your original parents, however, may not have escaped from the experience unscathed and you may also have grief which is yet to surface. I'm very glad to hear that you have good relationships with all your various family connections and it's good to see that you can accept that all of them have their place. Enjoy!

I did what I was told was 'the right thing' and waited until my adoptive parents had died before I searched for my original parents. By the time I found them, they were dead also. Now I realise that not only did I deny myself the opportunity to meet my original parents, I also denied them the opportunity to meet me and I denied my adoptive parents the opportunity to be involved in our reunion. Is it too late for me to do anything useful now?

It's very sad that you left it so late to search. Hopefully your experience can help others to think about their situation differently. There may be siblings for you to locate or there may be members of your original families who would be happy to meet you and who could provide you with information about your heritage and background. I hope you'll continue your search.

I'm adopted and I met my original parents and siblings, but I just didn't feel any connection with them. I feel a much greater sense of belonging in my adoptive family. Why do people make such a big deal about the biological connection?

We are all a combination of our ancestry and our environment. For those who have been adopted, ancestry and environment represent two different pathways. Many adopted people find it useful to contemplate the contribution that both may have made to their sense of identity.

I rang my original mother and introduced myself and she said that she hates me. How can she hate me when she has never met me?

It's interesting that she expresses such strong feelings towards you. She's clearly not indifferent to you! Adoption reunion situations tend to rekindle feelings of loss and grief related to the original separation. Hostility is a common component of grieving behaviour. What she hates at the moment, I suspect, is not you as a person, but the idea that you exist. She may hate and fear her history and her pain associated with that history. Fear of the truth and the impact of the truth on people's lives sometimes holds them back from getting involved in a reunion. It is very sad that people choose to live with lies and fear instead of openness and honesty. Hopefully she will not allow her current fear to prevent her from considering your generous offer of contact. I suggest that you allow her some time to consider and then make your offer again, perhaps by letter, which is less confronting. Hopefully, one day soon, she will recognise the depth of her feelings, decide to address them and feel ready to accept your offer.

I'm considering trying to find my original parents but I'm worried about how that might affect my adoptive parents. How do adoptive parents generally feel when their adopted children meet up with their original parents or other family members?

If you are a parent, you are aware as you are raising your children that when they are adults they will form their own relationships. If you have chosen to raise someone else's children (ie adopted children) then you will be aware that this may also include forming relationships with members of their families of origin. Many adoptive parents understand that the children they have adopted have been removed from their original families. They realise that reconnecting with them can be a valuable experience and see these relationships as a positive and desirable feature of their adopted child's life.

What do you think of the current use of surrogacy and anonymous donation of eggs and sperm?

Frankly, I'm horrified. I feel that such practices are not child-focussed but adult-focussed and that they will lead to many situations of genealogical bewilderment. Fortunately, adults who were created in these ways are now speaking out about the long term outcomes for them. It's very sad that some governments have not learned from people's adoption experiences and have allowed these situations to occur. Hopefully they will listen to the people who are personally affected and put a stop to them.

I've had problems throughout my life with drugs and alcohol and have been jailed more than once. I've seen so many psychologists, social workers and others who have tried to help me. However none of them was interested in the fact that I was adopted and told me that it wasn't relevant. Why won't they even consider it?

It's very sad to hear of your experience of so much ignorance among those in the helping professions. I suggest that the next time you attend for counselling, that you give your counsellor some useful reading material about the long term outcomes of adoption and ask her or him to think again.

Interpersonal Recovery

1. Interpersonal recovery and mourning

What is interpersonal recovery?

When something is lost and then found, it is often said to have been *recovered*. When an adoption takes place, a child and his or her families of origin are separated from each other. This separation means that losses are experienced. When family members who have been separated from each other by adoption find each other again and are reunited, therefore, they are, in a sense, *recovering* each other. This can be an opportunity to develop the relationships which were interrupted by the adoption. I have termed this 'interpersonal recovery'. Because interpersonal recovery work is a part of the adoption grieving process, it can give rise to intense emotional reactions. ***Interpersonal recovery is about addressing the long term impact on the relationships between family members who have been separated by adoption.***

Worden describes the tasks of mourning as firstly, to accept the reality of the loss, secondly, to work through the pain of grief, thirdly, to adjust to an environment in which the deceased is missing and fourthly, to relocate the deceased emotionally and move on with life (Worden, 1991, pp10-18). Worden's tasks were created to apply principally to grief following a bereavement, but they are readily transferable to other types of losses. In most cases of bereavement, these tasks would naturally follow on from the death. In an adoption situation, it is difficult to achieve the tasks of grieving at the time of separation and the reunion meeting can create the opportunity for those tasks to be experienced. I believe that those who seek reunion are attempting to create a situation in which they can experience these four tasks of mourning.

Task I – to accept the reality of the loss

When a reunion occurs there is a loss of fantasy, expectation and dreams. Reunion also confronts those involved with the reality of

129

the relationship which could have developed, had it not been for the adoption separation.

For some, reunion also brings about the loss of the comfortable position which they had created, in which they consoled themselves by taking the stance that the adoption separation had produced only positive outcomes and had not had any negative impact on their lives. Sometimes it is difficult for them to accept that this is not entirely the case.

Some people have difficulty accepting the reality which has replaced their previous position. This new reality is not always welcome. Often people can hardly believe that the reunion has actually happened, especially if they have been anticipating it for a long time, or, conversely, if they had never considered that it might one day happen. It can take on an aura of unreality. Some people try to avoid acknowledging the reality of the reunion by minimising the significance of the event.

Accepting the reality of the loss is not only an intellectual task but also an emotional one. Anger can be a feature of this acceptance; anger at the other party, anger at oneself, anger at others. Those who were not prepared for a reunion may be angry with the other party for causing it to happen. For those who do bring about a reunion, they may encounter a hostile response. Adopted people might be angry at their original parents for leaving them, angry at themselves for having enjoyed life regardless, angry at others for having colluded in it all. Original parents may be angry with themselves for allowing the adoption to happen, angry with others who engineered it and even angry with their child who may seem indifferent to them.

Mourning will be facilitated if there is an intellectual acceptance of the actual relationship between the two parties and also an emotional acceptance, which involves comprehending the implications of it all. Rituals, such as obtaining written evidence of the adoption or creating evidence of the reunion, for example with letters or photographs, can help with this task.

Some people report vivid dreams during adoption reunions. Dreams can be the subconscious mind's way of validating the reality of the event. Reunion, ie physically seeing and interacting with the other party, allows those involved to experience the reality of the loss by allowing them to confront the real person, rather than the image which they have created in their thoughts.

Accepting the reality of the loss involves understanding that a family was created when the child was born and that that family was prevented from developing when the child was adopted. There is no way of knowing what kind of family would have evolved, but accepting that the adoption has created a loss experience for all family members is the first step in working through the resultant grief.

Task II – to work through the pain of the grief

The first task leads, apparently inevitably, to the second. When those involved begin to understand the enormity of the loss which they have experienced, the pain of the grief resulting from that loss may begin to be felt. If those involved in the reunion are not prepared for pain, then they may experience a feeling of fear and panic and wish to withdraw from the reunion experience. This is sometimes viewed by others as 'running away'. It may, in fact, be an attempt to avoid pain, which is caused by a lack of understanding of the source and the purpose of the pain.

Seeking to avoid the pain, therefore, interrupts the grieving process and leaves the griever in a kind of limbo, not knowing which direction to take emotionally. Experiencing the pain of grief is a natural response to reunion, as it is a vital part of the grieving process. Failure to work through the pain of the grief may result in physical symptoms or in aberrant behaviour. Any attempt to avoid the pain may prolong the grieving.

Some people try to avoid the pain by shutting themselves down emotionally and refusing to allow the feelings to come to

131

the surface. Some use alcohol or drugs to suppress the pain. Some people move away geographically to avoid confronting the pain. Some have euphoric responses to reunion, but these are often fragile and short-lived. Sooner or later those who try to avoid grieving may be forced to confront it. It is more comfortable and productive to acknowledge the need to grieve and allow it to take its natural course, rather than to try to avoid it and then be at its mercy.

It can be difficult for members of the community who have not had personal experience of adoption to understand the concept of reunion-based grieving, as there is often the expectation that the reunion will be a joyful experience. People may be misled by contrived representations in the media of reunions, which appear to be the wonderfully happy end of the journey, rather than the opportunity to move forward and build relationships. It is rare for the long term outcomes of reunion to be portrayed. Grief experienced at the time of reunion, as at the time of separation, is often disenfranchised, because the losses which are highlighted and created by reunion are not openly acknowledged, publicly mourned or socially supported.

Task III – to adjust to the changed environment
Adjusting to the changed environment will be easier to accomplish if the first two tasks of grieving have been fully experienced and not avoided. For original parents, it is necessary for them to accept that the child whom they could have raised is now an adult and that their adult child has experienced a life which is entirely different from the one which might have been, had the adoption not taken place.

For the adopted person, it is necessary for them to accept that the parent who could have raised them has also experienced a life entirely different from the one which might have been, had the adoption not taken place. Both have had a life in which the impact of adoption has been crucial. The people they would have been, the relationships which would have grown and developed, are gone and can never be retrieved, just as if they had died.

An environment has been created by the adoption and that environment and its impact have to be accepted and the other, the lost opportunity, mourned, before progress can be made to the fourth task. It is impossible to predict how those involved will adjust to the new relationships which are created by the reunion experience, until it has happened. In the same way, it was impossible to know how original parents would feel about the separation from their child until after the birth had occurred. The environment has changed post-reunion and a considerable adjustment is needed. As with a bereavement, three months after the event is often a crucial time. The initial intensity has worn off and community interest has waned. It can be helpful to focus at that time on what has been gained from the change.

It helps also to confront what the reunion means for one's own sense of self. If a poor adjustment is made, the reunion event, like a bereavement '…can lead to intense repression where the bereaved perceive of themselves as helpless, inadequate, incapable, childlike or personally bankrupt' (Worden, 1991, p15). Some people feel that it is impossible for them to make that adjustment and they try to escape from it. Some feel that they have temporarily lost direction in life, until they have been able to make the necessary adjustment. Others work against themselves by promoting their own helplessness or by withdrawing from the world. Most, however, eventually move forward. Those who do not manage to achieve this task can be '…held prisoner by a dilemma…(they)…cannot solve' in a 'state of suspended growth' (Worden, 1991, p16).

Task IV – to move on with life
Moving on with life requires acceptance of what has occurred and a focus on the positive aspects of the current relationships in order for a degree of peace and contentment to be given an opportunity

to develop. If the three previous tasks have been fully experienced, there is hope that the moving on with life, which Worden proposes, can be successfully achieved. It is not reasonable to expect that the tasks of grieving will have been totally and finally experienced, however and there will always be times when the feelings undergone throughout the completion of those tasks will resurface. They can be experienced and accepted in the knowledge that they are a natural response to the reunion event and that they are manageable and will pass.

'Mourning ends when the mourner no longer has a need to reactivate the representation of the dead with exaggerated intensity in the course of daily living' (Worden, 1991, p16). In reunion, the task is to relocate the events of one's life and go forward with a sense of wholeness, without constantly wondering about what might have been. Adopted people and their original parents have had to shelve notions of their missing family members because of lack of knowledge. They can all come to understand that adoption is only one part of their lives. Not achieving this task would be trying to go back, to hold on to life as it was, as if the reunion had never happened. This could involve a return to secrecy and suppression of emotions and truth.

Adoption has been a mystery to many people who have not themselves had an adoption experience. It is often difficult for others to understand the depth of the impact of an adoption separation experience in people's lives. It is also difficult for others to understand the deep-seated reasons why those who have been separated from family members by adoption seek to be reunited with them.

I believe that I have discovered the missing piece of information, which solves that mystery. There exists a subconscious desire to complete the tasks of mourning in relation to the loss originally created by the adoption separation in order to be able to 'move on with life'.

2. Reunion grief

Why does reunion produce grief reactions?

Family reunions, whether connected to adoption or not, are generally portrayed as exciting, joyous events. Indeed, they often are joyous and thrilling. However, just as often, adoption reunions involve mixed feelings, which have seldom been anticipated and can therefore be distressing and confusing. Understanding why these feelings arise can make adoption reunions more enjoyable and manageable. The *ecstasy* of adoption reunions probably needs no explanation and is often enthusiastically anticipated. However, *agony* can also be experienced and this is often unexpected and alarming. Understanding how and why painful feelings and experiences occur around adoption reunions can make the whole experience more positive and productive.

I believe that the initial separation caused by the adoption creates a loss which results in a grief reaction. For many people this grief reaction is buried because they do not receive community support and understanding for their need to grieve. For some, there comes a time in their lives when they acknowledge this series of events and allow themselves to experience this grief. Sometimes this is done as a deliberate strategy, when someone decides to undertake personal recovery work, by exploring and acknowledging the impact of adoption separation on their lives. If personal recovery work has not been undertaken prior to reunion, however, the grief may spontaneously come to the surface, without any planning or preparation on the part of the person involved.

The reactions to contact from a family member of those who have been unaware of any buried grief are very revealing. Throughout our lives it is not uncommon to be contacted by people who are strangers to us. This occurs for a variety of reasons, but rarely causes severe distress of any kind. It is rare for deep emotions to result from a contact by a person who is

135

unknown to us. Contact from family members from whom one has been separated by adoption, on the other hand, often results in extreme emotional reactions. Responses which are common to such situations are anger, joy, sadness, relief and sometimes a lack of reaction which could be described as numbness.

These responses often occur in situations where those contacted claim not to have been aware of any emotional impact of adoption on their lives, prior to the contact. In my experience, it is highly unlikely that contact from a person who is, in a sense, unknown, could, in itself, *create* such dramatic responses. I believe that the contact actually *awakens* feelings which have been buried and have therefore been, until that moment, unacknowledged.

Many, who had previously claimed not to have suffered from the impact of adoption in their lives, find that the contact itself allows feelings, which they were not aware that they had, to come to the surface. I believe that this is a positive, productive step in the process of coming to terms with one's adoption experience and assimilating it into one's life. Releasing that buried grief allows people to move forward and grow in self-knowledge.

The reunion itself is a major recovery event and is therefore an important part of the process of healing. If the grief, which has been dormant since the separation, has already been addressed through personal recovery work, then the reunion may feel more manageable and the impact of the reunion event may be less marked. If the grief has not been addressed, then it may have become chronic. I believe that this is why many reunion experiences resemble bereavement situations and can cause major grieving behaviour to be exhibited.

When the original loss occurred (ie the separation caused by adoption), neither party was able to perform the tasks of mourning. Those people who later seek reunion have, albeit sometimes subconsciously, recognised that they are suffering from delayed or chronic grief and are attempting to give themselves the opportunity to work through those grieving tasks. What then seems to happen is, that when the reunion occurs, this event echoes the original loss event, by highlighting the lost opportunity to spend those intervening years together. This may precipitate grieving, as if the loss had just occurred. Reunion becomes, in that way, a trigger for the grieving that was not able to take place at the time of the initial loss. This explains why reunion so often results in emotions which are similar to those which follow a bereavement ie sadness, numbness, a sense of unreality, anger, guilt and fear.

Unfortunately, few people are aware of the nature of reunion grief and there is an expectation in the community that the reunion will be an event to be enjoyed and celebrated. Many reunions are, of course, times of great joy and celebration. It can be difficult, therefore, for those affected by reunion grief to find a way to express it and manage it. I believe that when there is a wider understanding of the reasons why reunions can result in grief reactions, then those who are experiencing a reunion will be able to receive more support and acceptance, both from those close to them and from professionals working with them.

Anticipatory grief at the time of reunion

Raphael describes anticipatory grief, indicating that those who are anticipating a bereavement go through phases of denial, angry protest and acceptance (Raphael, 1983, pp50-53). Many fluctuate between phases and the degree of acceptance varies from time to time. People tend to hold on to what is familiar and resent the impending change. One emotion may be prominent. It could be anger, sadness, regret, resentment or guilt (Raphael, 1983, p396).

The first response to news that death is inevitable is usually shock, numbness, disbelief, denial as well as a sense of unreality. This shock must be absorbed. Raphael believes that the way that the news is broken is important. It can be done in an

137

'assaultive' way, leaving the person traumatised and distressed by the experience, as well as by the news. Once the acceptance has set in, then come fear, anxiety, helplessness, angry protest and resentment. Denial may reappear at any time. This can force people to confront past guilt and they may withdraw from the world into themselves. It often causes people to review their lives. Raphael says that with a forthcoming bereavement, the signs of anticipatory grief are sadness, fear, anger, distress, guilt, sorrow, despair and depression. When the death occurs, the principal sensation is often relief. Regardless of the anticipation, however, the actual death will usually trigger grieving.

These emotions can also occur in those who have been in contact with a lost family member and for whom a reunion is a possibility. Anticipating a reunion is in many ways similar to anticipating a death. At the time of contact, before the reunion has occurred, many exhibit denial. There are also many angry protests. Often these phases are followed by acceptance. It is impossible to determine how long each of these phases may last. I have known people to remain in denial, sometimes combined with angry protest, for many years. Some eventually move on to the acceptance phase.

In some cases, the other party wearies of waiting for this to happen and precipitates a reunion (eg by arriving at the other person's home unannounced) to try to force the family member involved to enter the acceptance phase. As with anticipating a bereavement, some appear to have reached acceptance, only to slip back sometimes into one of the other phases. Some people are resistant to change and choose to avoid acceptance for as long as they are able.

As with the first response to the fact that a death is inevitable, the first response to contact from a family member from whom one has been separated is often shock, followed by numbness, disbelief and denial. It can take time for the initial shock to be absorbed. As with news of an impending death, it is

138

important how the news of reunion contact is broken. In some cases, very tactless and insensitive approaches have caused people to stay for longer in the shock phase than would be considered comfortable. Once the person has absorbed the shock and reached a level of acceptance of the situation, then fear is often the predominant emotion. Fear of a possible change in a relationship can cause people to hold on to feelings of helplessness and resentment. As with anticipation of a death, denial can recur at any time and can be used as a 'comfort zone' to avoid confronting the reality of the impact of the contact. As with a death, regardless of the anticipation, the actual reunion often triggers grieving.

Normal grief reactions

Worden describes characteristics of normal grief following a bereavement (Worden, 1991, p22). Similar behaviour is also common in adoption reunion circumstances. Sometimes those involved are puzzled by their feelings and behaviour, as they have no clear understanding of why they occur. They are, in fact, components of normal grieving behaviour and when people understand that reunion creates the atmosphere for the grieving of the adoption separation to occur, they see that their reactions are grieving reactions and, as such, are exactly what one would expect to occur.

The characteristics outlined by Worden are:

Bodily distress ~ Many of those who experience an adoption reunion find themselves frequently tearful and anxious or suffering from insomnia, indigestion and other physical features suggesting anguish.
Preoccupation with the deceased ~ Many describe thinking about the reunion frequently and for some people the relationship has some of the elements of a love affair.

Guilt ~ Reunion often causes feelings of guilt to surface for original parents when they are confronted with the reality of the separation of the child from the family, while some adopted adults also feel guilty that they seem to have been the cause of so much distress to their parents.

Hostility ~ Hostility is a common feature of adoption reunions and sometimes takes the form of refusal of contact.

Inability to function as one had before the loss ~ For many people the reunion experience seems to 'take over' their lives for a period of time and they sometimes describe their reaction to the reunion as verging on 'obsessive'.

Worden also lists other feelings which are manifestations of normal grief, which are also common in adoption reunions (Worden, 1991, p22):

Sadness ~ When reunion occurs, many people feel an overwhelming sense of sadness but cannot explain exactly why they are so sad.

Loneliness ~ Many who are experiencing reunion feel isolated and have a sense that no one else understands and often find that support groups can be very helpful, as can reading of the experiences of others.

Fatigue ~ The reunion experience can be very emotionally draining and this can lead to physical exhaustion, which may result in an appearance of apathy or listlessness.

Helplessness ~ The reunion experience can be so overwhelming that some people just feel unable to cope and become very dependent and needy.

Shock ~ No matter how well prepared people think they are for the reunion event, the reality of it often results in a sense of shock.

Numbness ~ After a bereavement, or a reunion, people may experience an emotional numbness, which can be a protective mechanism against feelings which may seem overwhelming.

Anger ~ Anger is considered to be a manifestation of normal grief. Confronting the reality of the adoption separation frequently engenders feelings of anger. Worden talks about the child who became separated from his mother in the shopping centre. He experienced fear and anxiety, but when she returned to him, rather than expressing love and relief, the child displayed anger and 'kicked her in the shins'. Worden says that this is the child's way of saying, *Don't leave me again!*

Adopted people often express anger towards their original parents when they are reunited with them, or when they are offered the opportunity to reunite. This reaction is similar to that described by Worden of the child separated from his mother. When the reunion occurs, or when reunion is offered, the adopted adult is reminded that they were 'left' by the parents as an infant and their anger at this separation comes to the surface. This anger causes some adopted adults to refuse reunion. For some adopted people, the fact that they were adopted suggests to them that they were unlovable. When someone claims to love them, they may exhibit challenging behaviour as a way of testing this claim.

For original parents, the anger is often displaced or directed towards some other person, often blaming them for the adoption. The line of reasoning is that if someone can be blamed, then they are responsible and hence the loss could have been prevented (Worden, 1991, p23). Some people direct anger against themselves and become depressed or even suicidal.

It is important to remember that these are all normal components of grieving experiences and that their intensity reduces with time. When someone dies, for example, others would consider it normal for us to be tearful for a period of time. It is also considered normal for a bereaved person to be preoccupied with the deceased for some time. When we realise that adoption reunion precipitates a grieving experience, then it becomes clear that this behaviour is also 'normal' in reunion circumstances.

141

Complicated grief and adoption reunion

According to Worden, if mourning is not undertaken, grief can become 'complicated' (Worden, 1991, pp71-77). Worden describes complicated grief reactions under four headings: chronic grief reactions, delayed grief reactions, exaggerated grief reactions and masked grief reactions. Adopted people and their original parents may exhibit signs of all four complicated grief reactions.

Chronic ~ A chronic grief reaction is one that is excessive in duration ie it lasts for an unexpectedly long time after the loss has occurred. Sometimes those who have experienced an adoption separation seem to carry a deep sadness for many years. Overt sadness around holidays and anniversaries can also be a sign of a chronic grief situation.

Delayed ~ A delayed grief reaction is one in which the emotional reaction experienced at the time of the loss has not been sufficient to the loss. This kind of grief reaction is also known as an inhibited, suppressed or postponed grief reaction. Adopted people and their original parents sometimes react excessively to subsequent losses in their lives, because they have not been able to process adequately the loss associated with the separation which occurred at the time of the adoption.

Exaggerated ~ An exaggerated grief reaction is one in which the person experiences the intensification of a normal grief reaction and feels overwhelmed by it. This can result in a type of grieving behaviour which is excessive and disabling and which can develop into psychiatric conditions, such as clinical depression and anxiety disorders. Substance abuse in adulthood can also be a feature of this type of grief reaction.

Masked ~ A masked grief reaction is one in which people experience symptoms and behaviour which cause them difficulty, but they do not recognise that these are related to the loss which they have experienced. The symptoms which they develop are

142

known as 'equivalents of grief'. Masked grief may be a self-protection mechanism, used to circumvent the grief process. The symptoms can be physical (unexplained pain or discomfort of some kind) or emotional (depression or acting-out behaviour). Some people mask their grief with intense activity. Such activity is common following bereavement. There are many whose lives have been affected by adoption separation, who expend intense energy on their careers. This may be a way of circumventing the grief process by keeping themselves so busy that they have no time to mourn.

Another consequence of complicated grief can be the avoidance of further close attachments in order to ensure that another grief experience does not occur, if relationships come to an end for any reason. Some adopted adults appear to be emotionally detached and do not form long term relationships as adults, preferring to remain unattached. This kind of reaction has also prevented many parents who have been separated from children through adoption from having subsequent children.

When a reunion occurs, it can present an opportunity for those involved to complete the tasks of mourning and recover from the effects of the complicated grief which may have been with them since the separation. Many find that after experiencing reunion, they are better able to cope with subsequent losses in their lives.

How is reunion grief expressed?

Reunion grief can express itself in many forms, as does grief following a bereavement. Not everyone experiences the same intensity of pain or feels it in the same way. For some the main emotion is anger and this has not always been recognised as a grief reaction. Many have been puzzled by the degree of hostility expressed when family members have been offered the opportunity of contact. For those who do not understand that hostility is a common component of grief, some of the responses

143

experienced can appear to be alarmingly extreme. However, when this hostility is viewed in a grief perspective, it becomes more comprehensible.

Anyone who has been present in a hospital ward, for example, where an unexpected death has occurred, may have witnessed much anger and hostility as the bereaved struggle to accept the reality of what has happened. Often there is a search for someone to blame and a desire to make some sense of what has happened by making accusations. Similar behaviour may occur at the time of contact between family members separated by adoption. Anger and sadness sometimes come to the surface and there is sometimes a desire to blame and accuse. Bereavement, especially when it is unexpected, can cause a deep sense of injustice and resentment. So too can adoption contact and reunion. In both cases, those affected are actually angry at the event, but they often direct their anger at the people involved. For original parents, their sense of loss tends to increase dramatically at the time of reunion. With adopted people it seems more common that their anger increases suddenly at the time of reunion. When these feelings are understood and acknowledged, there is no need for them to prevent a relationship from developing.

As with any grieving experience, a person who is experiencing an adoption reunion will not necessarily go through an identifiable series of stages of grieving in a clearly consecutive manner. Emotions will fluctuate. Sadly, expectations are raised and it is difficult to deal with what may appear to be regression. There may come a time when one party feels fairly comfortable in the relationship and has certain expectations of behaviour. The other party may then resort to either angry outbursts or long silences which often involve blaming, accusations and insults. While this kind of behaviour would always be distressing, it is often more difficult to accept if it occurs at a later stage in the relationship than it might have been earlier.

144

Managing the reunion

The reunion is in some ways a ritual event in itself and is often planned to some extent in the way that a funeral service is planned. The venue and the participants are selected, the date and time is set and personal preparations are made. It can be distressing and disconcerting for a reunion to be planned to take place in the presence of observers, or for photographs or film footage to be taken without consent. It is wise to be considerate so as not to sabotage the reunion from the outset.

In adoption reunion situations, as well as at funerals, some people repress their emotions in public, by downplaying the importance of the event and their emotional reaction to it, in order to try to conceal their vulnerability. At the time of reunion, it can be hurtful if one party overtly minimises the importance of the meeting and the relationship.

As with grieving a bereavement, there are crucial points in time at which people can feel overwhelmed after a reunion. Three months after the event is often a time when the grievers can go through a crisis. At this stage in the mourning process, the community generally withdraws the level of support which was provided immediately after the loss event, resulting in a feeling in the mourners of being unable to manage their experience. In adoption reunion situations this may be the time at which one party withdraws temporarily from the relationship, finding it overwhelming. An awareness that this is a common response in grieving behaviour can help those affected to be patient and understanding.

Anniversaries of the event are often challenging. It is useful to mark the first anniversary of the reunion in some way which acknowledges its significance. Other challenging events are family occasions such as birthdays.

3. Reunion outcomes

Understanding the purpose of reunion

Those who have had no experience of adoption are generally not aware of the feelings experienced by those who have. In fact, the general community often finds itself baffled by the reasons behind the efforts of those who have been separated from family members through adoption to achieve reunion. It is my belief that the wish to reunite is part of the awareness, although often subconscious, of the fact that there exists a grief which has not been addressed. I believe that those who attempt to create a reunion experience have a deep-seated desire for emotional wholeness, which leads them in that direction and that reunion plays a major role in the process of mourning adoption losses. I believe that desiring reunion is a positive sign, as it is a striving for openness, growth and healing.

Because they are not consciously seeking grief, however, many people are shocked and dismayed when the reunion leads to painful grieving experiences. It is important to be aware that *the reunion does not create the grief.* The grief is caused by the initial separation, although that grief is often not experienced until the reunion takes place.

There is also, however, a loss which is experienced when reunion occurs. Reunion represents the loss of ignorance and fear. Reunion can replace ignorance with knowledge and fear with confidence. While learning the truth may create a temporary situation of unrest, it is also a great opportunity for growth. At the time of reunion, original parents sometimes mourn the loss of the child that they could have raised, while adopted people may mourn the loss of the self that might have been.

Those who seek reunion rarely have a clear understanding of their hopes and expectations. Many say that they did not know why they were seeking reunion until after it occurred and that the reunion produced outcomes which they could never have predicted. For many, it is only after the reunion occurs that connections between certain events in their lives are made.

One of the principal issues in the unresolved grief which follows adoption separation, is the lack of finality of the loss. With a death, there is eventually no option to the mourners but to accept that the deceased is unavailable. With an adoption separation, there is always the possibility of a reunion. This possibility is one of the factors which inhibits the grieving process and often means that the grief remains unresolved.

I believe that many of those who have experienced an adoption separation are seeking a form of grief resolution. One way to try to achieve this is to create a situation which represents this finality, which has been missing from the adoption separation experience. I believe that this desire for finality and therefore for a full grieving experience, leads many people to seek a reunion. The reunion is in some ways a mirror image of the original separation. Reunion represents the closing of the circle of separation which began at the time of the adoption.

The reunion is able to take the place of the finality which we associate with death and which is missing from adoption separation situations. The reunion is the death of hopes and fears, the death of wondering and imagining and the beginning of facing reality. For many, although their grief has been present since the original separation, it has been to a large extent unexpressed and perhaps even unacknowledged. Some have been able to express their grief prior to reunion and to have it acknowledged and validated. For them the reunion allows them to proceed further down the path of grief resolution. For many people, however, their grieving begins at the moment of reunion, when they are confronted with the reality and the finality of their loss.

The family relationship between the original mother and her child is central to adoption. My description of adoption separation and reunion charts the journey from the *disintegration* of a family due to adoption, to the *reintegration* of the lost family

147

members into each other's lives. When reunion is being considered, therefore, the two principal parties must be the original mother and the adult adopted child, although there can be great value in having other members of the family, including the father, siblings and grandparents, actively involved.

Many original mothers have 'buried' their lost children emotionally and then 'resurrected' them when the time was appropriate. These mothers know deep inside that if they ever meet their children again, that those children will be unrecognisable compared with how they looked when their mothers last saw them (if, indeed, they did see their children) and so they have to be prepared, in a sense, for a new 'incarnation' of their child.

For some original parents, it is difficult for them to merge the two facets of their child's identity – the baby and the adult. Original mothers have been known to bring gifts to their adult child at the time of reunion, which would be appropriate to a young child, such as blankets and soft toys. These are also gifts which have a comforting function. Many original mothers have a strong desire at the time of reunion to hold and touch their children. The adult child may not feel comfortable with such behaviour, however and it would be wise for these mothers to be cautious and to take their lead from their children.

What happens when the child is an adult is that it is as if they have been lost and then re-found. This is similar to the tradition in some societies of having a public burial after a death, followed by the welcoming of the deceased back, as one of the ancestors. In this way the deceased takes on a new and very clear role. This could be viewed as being a healthier way of dealing with death than emotionally 'holding on' to the deceased in their former role and therefore having difficulty accepting that, in that role, they are gone forever.

Interpersonal recovery, like personal recovery, has both an intellectual element (replacing ignorance with knowledge) and an emotional element (replacing fear with confidence). The intellectual element involves the exchange of information. Original parents are able to inform their adopted adult children of the circumstances which led to their adoption and adopted adults are able to inform their original parents of the events which have occurred in their lives since the adoption. Adopted adults may have previously been given erroneous information. Their original parents seldom have received any information at all. The meeting itself, as well as the exchange of information, may bring many emotions to the surface.

Why some people refuse reunion

It is unwise to make any assumptions in a potential reunion situation. The person who makes the first contact has no way of knowing how far the other party has gone in processing and experiencing their grief. Even being the one who makes the contact does not necessarily mean that you are at an appropriate stage in your healing to accommodate the reunion well. It is always important to remember that you do not have the power to change the other person and that, in some respects, you will have to accept them as they are. Although a reunion by definition involves two parties, it may only have been sought by one party. In such cases, the invitation from one party to be part of a reunion is often an invitation to the other party to begin acknowledging their loss and experiencing their grief.

All of those who know that they have been separated from a family member by adoption choose whether or not to prepare themselves for the possibility of reunion. In some ways the situation is similar to facing the deaths of our parents. We all know that there is a strong likelihood that we will experience the deaths of our parents, whether we wish to or not. This means that we cannot honestly say, when this occurs, that we 'never thought this would happen'. Similarly, although many people have chosen not to prepare themselves for the possibility of adoption reunion, they cannot genuinely claim, if it does occur, that it has taken them totally by surprise.

Some people do not respond well to an invitation to be part of a reunion, because they are at a place in their life where they feel it necessary to concentrate on their own needs. They may not be willing to introduce the reunion factor into their current situation. They may feel that all of their energies are being used already and that they do not have the inner resources to confront the reunion issue. For them, it may be a question of postponing a reunion until what seems like a more appropriate time.

Sometimes original parents refuse to accept adult adopted children into their lives because they feel guilty and ashamed, not of the child, but of themselves. Sometimes adopted adults refuse to accept their original parents into their lives because they feel more comfortable minimising the impact of adoption on their lives and do not wish to make themselves vulnerable by exploring it. In situations such as these, those affected are not 'rejecting' the other party but rather are choosing not to proceed with their healing at that time. This is where some personal recovery work could be very valuable.

People sometimes say that they choose not to seek out a lost family member, because of fear of 'disruption'. They fear either the disruption to their own life or causing disruption to the life of the other party. In fact, our lives are made up of 'disruptions' – falling in love, having a child, taking a holiday, moving house, starting a new job. Many of these 'disruptions' are viewed in a positive light and, indeed, are considered to be expected elements of adult life. The sort of disruption you may cause, if you contact a family member from whom you have been separated by adoption, is the opportunity to address issues which have been buried and have perhaps been causing them stress and anxiety. This is actually a 'disruption' which has the potential to have a very positive outcome.

150

Many people fear a reunion because it is a step into the unknown; it is a step from which there is no stepping back. They fear that this event will change their lives forever. People often fear grief and it can take courage to make a deliberate decision to confront one's grief. When people make statements like *I couldn't cope with it* or *I'm not interested*, often what they mean is, that they fear the impact of the grief and they know that dealing with it will be difficult and so they are choosing to avoid confronting it. If reunion is delayed, it is often a sign that the issues created by the adoption separation have not been addressed. There are many instances where one party is unprepared for reunion and their grieving and healing begin only after contact has been made.

The word 'interfere' also crops up frequently in discussion about adoption reunions. Interference occurs in adoptions because a child is adopted only after there has been interference with the initial bond between mother and child. It is that original interference which creates the need for recovery, of which reunion is such a large part. Suggesting that someone become involved in a reunion is not interfering; it is inviting. It is part of adulthood to consider invitations and either to accept or refuse them. Being invited to take part in an event is not generally viewed as interference.

Some people refuse to agree to be involved in a reunion because they claim to be concerned about the impact on others. In trying to take on responsibility for the feelings of others, however, they may be using this as an excuse for their own fear. Some of those affected by adoption separation lost the ability to trust their own feelings, when they were told that their feelings of grief resulting from the separation were inappropriate. They then find it difficult to deal with the option of contact.

Some adopted people refuse contact with their original parents as a way of expressing their anger with them. They refuse to respond to invitations as a way of punishing the original parents and exercising control over the situation. Sometimes they claim to

151

be protecting their adoptive parents. Original parents sometimes refuse contact out of fear, or out of anger with the whole experience. They also sometimes claim to be protecting others such as their other children or their partner. Rather than protecting others, such behaviour can deny them the opportunity to grow, to learn and to show generosity.

At the Sixth Australian Conference on Adoption, Sarah Berryman reported on research into adoption reunions and their effects on people's lives which had been undertaken at the Post Adoption Resource Centre in New South Wales. The researchers interviewed eighty-one people who had used the centre to mediate on their behalf. They found that a majority of 'searchers' and, interestingly, an even larger majority of 'found' people described the reunion relationship in entirely positive or in largely positive terms and that although 59% of those who had been found reported that they had not planned to search for family members, eighty of the eighty-one people interviewed had no regrets about the reunion (Berryman, 1997, p306).

Will the reunion 'work out'?

Some people talk of reunions between family members who have been separated by adoption in terms of 'success' and 'failure'. I feel that this is an inappropriate and unhelpful way of looking at this complex situation. There are often family members, who have been part of the same family, who, as adults, choose not to spend time together. No one considers describing their relationships as having 'failed'. We simply accept that we cannot choose our relatives and that we do not always have much in common with them, nor enjoy spending time in their company. As adults we make those choices. Regardless of our choices, however, nothing changes the fact that we are related.

Some people expect the person with whom they are to be reunited to do the recovery work for them. It is, in fact, the experience of reunion, not the person with whom you are reunited, which aids recovery. It is important to remember that people are responsible for their own recovery, regardless of whether or not a reunion takes place or whether or not it meets their expectations. The family member with whom you are reunited is not responsible for providing you with what you need to recover. Everyone can achieve a degree of personal recovery regardless of their reunion opportunities. Your relative may or may not appreciate your needs and your experience. Regardless of how much or how little they have to offer, you can use the experience of reunion to aid your recovery.

It is helpful for anyone contemplating a reunion if they have made some effort to know and understand themselves, before attempting to get to know or understand the other person. Personal recovery work will help people to get to know themselves better. It can be a preparation for reunion but it can also be useful in its own right for those who never have a reunion.

If you are considering initiating a reunion, then it is wise to bear in mind that the person you are hoping to meet may not have conducted any preparation for reunion and may need some time to come to terms with the reality of it.

Many have wondered why, in some reunion situations, contact continues for some time and then ceases. This can happen because, after reunion has taken place, some people want to go back. It often happens when a death occurs, that a survivor might wish that things could go back to the way they were before, when they were able to spend time with the lost one and look forward to a future with them. They wish that the death had never happened, as life was pleasanter before.

For some who experience an adoption reunion, they also would like to go back to the way life was before it happened. Life may have seemed simpler then and more comfortable and so they cut off from the other party, as if they had never met and try to get back to the comfortable place which they had inhabited, before they confronted the reality that reunion provides. It is not possible,

153

of course, to undo a reunion experience, any more than it is possible to reverse a bereavement experience. *Trying to move back, by definition, prevents people from moving forward.*

Unknown factors
Each party to an adoption reunion is bringing with them certain unknown issues. Any or all of these can give rise to difficulties in the reunion.

Grief ~ You have no way of knowing to what extent the other party has recognised or experienced their grief. It is wise not to underestimate the depth of this grief, even though it may not be immediately apparent.

Experience ~ The other party may already have had experiences with family members, or even with partners or friends, which have resulted in apprehension or issues of trust. They may have been mistreated or they may have been indulged. On the basis of this, they may have certain expectations around the reunion.

Values ~ Values and beliefs are very important to how we view the world and our place in it. People's values vary widely and sometimes differences in religious or moral beliefs can cause conflict. Personal qualities valued by one person may be of no importance to another. This can lead to disappointment and anxiety. It is important to remember the need for acceptance and honesty in reunion relationships.

Knowledge ~ Some people take time and trouble to prepare themselves for reunion by reading, talking and reflecting. Others go into a reunion with absolutely no awareness of the issues which underlie adoption separation and reunion.

Emotions ~ Reunion is a very emotional time and some emotions may seem to be unreasonable or frightening. It can be useful to find an outlet for these emotions which will not damage the reunion relationship.

Personality ~ Even in families where there has been no adoption, children often have very different personalities from each other and from their parents. It takes time to familiarise yourself with someone's personal characteristics.

Intentions ~ Sadly, some people precipitate a reunion with the intention of punishing and may thereby cause pain. Others focus solely on what it is that they want from the reunion and show no concern for its impact on the other party.

Expectations ~ The parent and child may have been told that their feelings around the adoption separation are not valid. They may both have learned not to trust and may have lost faith in their ability to respond appropriately to emotional issues in their lives. It is wise not to go into a reunion with unrealistic expectations.

Reunion outcomes

Grief processing and the performance of mourning tasks have been described in various forms by many who have written about grief issues. In relation to processing the grief resulting from an adoption separation, I believe that the reunion experience can be very valuable. In my view there are four possible reunion outcomes in relation to grief processing.

There are those who choose not to attempt to bring about a reunion. These people have, in my opinion, either not begun to perform the mourning tasks, or else their progress through these tasks has been arrested at some point, short of seeking reunion.

There are others who experience reunion and resist performing the mourning tasks and so do not take the opportunity presented by reunion to address their issues of loss. For them the loss remains an on-going unresolved issue.

A third group desire a reunion but are unable to achieve it, because the other party remains unavailable to them. This can be as a result of death, refusal or simply the failure to locate the person sought. I believe that even when a physical reunion is not possible, a great deal can be achieved in the area of personal recovery. Confronting and acknowledging the impact of the loss in one's life and celebrating the positive aspects of one's experience can be useful, even if no reunion takes place.

There are those who experience reunion and, as a result of that experience, they are able to perform the mourning tasks and incorporate the adoption experience into their lives. Happily, there are many families in which close, strong bonds are formed after reunion and these can enrich and enhance the lives of all the family members involved.

Regardless of the reunion outcome, most people find that they are glad to have faced their fears and survived. Questions are answered, mysteries are solved and many people feel a sense of personal satisfaction.

I believe that reunion can provide a great opportunity for healing to those who have been separated by adoption, by giving them the opportunity to process their grief and move forward. It is my considered opinion, therefore, that governments have a responsibility to enact legislation that will make the experience of reunion accessible to as many people as possible and provide services which will support people through the reunion experience.

4a. Questions asked by adoptive parents

Why don't you talk about the way adoptive parents experience reunion?

Adoption reunions are about reuniting family members who have been separated from each other by adoption. Adoptive parents do not experience reunions, unless they have been separated from a family member by adoption. When someone does experience an adoption reunion, this can alter their view of themselves and their life to a considerable degree. This may then have an impact on the way that they relate to those who are close to them, such as their parents, partners or children. It can be helpful for those people to provide support and understanding.

I may be an adoptive mother but I'm the only mother my adopted daughter has ever known. Why should I be cast aside just because her original mother has decided to come into her life after I was the one who did all the work to raise her?

Sadly, adoptive parents sometimes complain that they feel as if they have been only 'temporary care-givers' who are then 'cast aside' when the 'real' parents come back into their adopted child's life. The role of any parent is to be a temporary care-giver – to care for children until those children become adults and are able to care for themselves. The only parents whose care-giving role continues past the age of adulthood of their children are parents whose children have a disability which prevents them from taking full responsibility for their own care. In most families, if we raise our children effectively, then we expect that our care will no longer be required when they become adults. In healthy, secure relationships between adoptive parents and their adopted children, an adult child's relationship with their families of origin is not viewed as a threat to the relationship between the adoptive parents and the adult adopted child.

I'm an adoptive parent and our adopted son has no interest in finding his original families. I'm disappointed and feel as if we've failed him. Where did we go wrong?

You are not responsible for the decisions he makes. You can reassure him that you feel that it would be in his best interests to seek out his original families and that you will be happy to support him in this. However, he needs to do this when he feels ready. Confronting the truth about the place of adoption separation in our lives requires a degree of courage. Seeking a reunion requires a spirit of generosity. Many people will only proceed when they are able to overcome any anxiety they may feel about confronting the truth.

Our adopted daughter searched for her original parents and met them and we weren't allowed to share this experience with her, because she did it all behind our backs. We were very hurt by her actions. Wouldn't it have been better for her to be open and honest about what she was doing?

When our children become adults, there are many parts of their lives which they choose not to share with their parents. I'm sure that there are aspects of your lives that you have chosen not to share with your parents. This is generally considered to be quite appropriate. Sometimes adopted adults do not include their adoptive parents in their reunion plans because they fear their disapproval or because they fear their interference. Sometimes, however, it's just that they feel the need to experience reunion alone without outside influences. It's their experience and they need to feel a sense of ownership of what's happening and to feel confident that they are managing it in their own way. If you had a healthy relationship with your daughter before her reunion, then it's unlikely that this will be adversely affected by her having contact with her original parents. In fact, the opposite is usually the case. After reunion, adopted adults usually feel more comfortable with themselves and therefore are better able to

158

relate to other people. However, for many people the reunion is an emotional trauma and it can take time for those emotions to settle. It would be helpful for your adopted daughter if you can try to understand her experience and support her through it.

I don't understand why people describe meetings between adults who were adopted as children and members of their original families as 'reunions'. The children we adopted never knew their original parents and so if they decide to meet them, they will be meeting them for the first time. How can this be considered a 'reunion'?

A mother and child are intimately connected during pregnancy and childbirth, regardless of what happens after the child is born. Mothers and children who are separated after the birth and meet again later in life are being reunited. Some babies who were subsequently adopted spent time before the adoption with other family members, for example, fathers, grandparents etc. In other situations, they are meeting people for the first time. However, when adults who were adopted as children meet any member of their original families, they are being reunited with their original identities.

Our adopted daughter was perfectly happy and settled until her original mother came back into her life. Now we never see her. This reunion has ruined our lives. Wouldn't it have been better if it hadn't happened?

It's very sad that you feel that your daughter's reunion with her mother has 'ruined' your lives. When you chose to raise another couple's child, you knew that when that child was an adult, she would develop other relationships. This is a part of growing up. Our adult children choose how much time they wish to spend with us. It seems that, at this time in her life, your adopted daughter is putting a lot of time and energy into building a relationship with her original mother. It is normal for such relationships to feel all-consuming in the early stages. Is it really so hard to accept that, when you have already had all those years with her? Can you be generous enough to share her now with her original parents? As adoptive parents, you can support your adopted daughter and show that you understand the significance for her of reconnecting with family members and assist your adopted daughter to work through the issues which this reunion is raising for her. If you had a close relationship with your adopted daughter before she was reunited with her original mother, then there is no reason for that closeness to be lost, just because there are now more people in her life who are important to her. I'm sure, if you are patient and understanding, this will become clear.

We never lied about the fact that our children were adopted, but we didn't think it was necessary for the children to be constantly reminded of it. In what ways do you find that adoptive parents fail to acknowledge the truth about their adopted children's origins?

Sometimes this happens by default; for example, failing to correct others when they assume that the children have inherited certain characteristics or will inherit certain characteristics from their adoptive parents. This can, in fact, be an opportunity to state the truth and show the child that there is no shame attached to the fact that they are not related by blood to their adoptive parents. I met one adoptive parent, for example, who introduced me to his adopted son with the comment that the son clearly took 'his good looks from his mother' (referring to the adoptive mother). Deliberately stating such untruths with regard to an adopted child can give the message to the child that their adopted status is something shameful and must be concealed. This is not likely to foster a good self-image in the child.

I'm afraid that if my adopted son finds out the truth about his origins, that it will ruin his life. Surely, in some situations, it's better for people not to know?

160

The truth offers an opportunity of living authentically and confronting reality. The truth may cause life to seem more complex than it had previously appeared, but, in actual fact, often it was the previous deceit and/or ignorance which caused the difficulties, not the revelation of the truth. Knowingly withholding the truth from someone (ie an adult) is making a choice on their behalf instead of allowing them to make their own decisions. It may be difficult for you to allow your son to make his own decisions, but, as an adult, that is what he must learn to do. I hope that you'll have faith in him to manage the outcomes.

I have met the original mother of my adopted daughter and I told her that I thought she had done the right thing in giving up her child. Her action gave me the joy of raising a child and allowed me to give that child everything she needed in life. How could any mother not think that that was the right thing to do?

I don't think it's about whether it was the right thing or the wrong thing do to. If the child had a happy life does that mean that the mother did the right thing? If the child had an unhappy life does that mean that the mother did the wrong thing? It's not possible to judge the action by its consequences, as they were unknown at the time. In my opinion, it is more useful to judge the action on its motives. The mother had no way of knowing what the outcome was going to be, either for herself or for her child. For many mothers, their pain and their loss were devalued because they were being told that they were doing 'the right thing'. It may have seemed 'right' for you, but the adoption separation has had long-term implications for both your adopted daughter and her original mother.

We raised three adopted children and gave them everything we could because their original parents didn't want to bring them up. How can it be right for their original parents to come into our lives and try to take their children back?

161

It's not possible to 'take back' an adult child. Our adult children don't belong to us. Once our children reach adulthood, they form adult relationships. For adopted children, those relationships may include members of their original families. Having relationships with relatives is a normal part of life and your adult children will choose for themselves which people they wish to include in their lives. Many adopted adults have on-going contact with members of their original families, as well as members of their adoptive families. They can manage to make room for everyone, if they are prepared to make the effort.

As adoptive parents, we were told that we would never hear from the original parents of our adopted children after the adoptions took place. Surely it's unfair that they have changed the rules and that original parents now are making contact with their children?

Regardless of what anyone was told to expect, the fact is that the children you adopted have other families. In spite of the secrecy and denial that have taken place, all adoptive parents know that they have chosen to raise someone else's child. All adoptive parents know that their adopted child has other families and all adoptive parents know that one day there could be a reunion between that child and members of his or her original families. Some have chosen to anticipate and prepare themselves and the child whom they have adopted for the possibility of that event and some have not. When policies and practices are seen to be inequitable and unjust, it is right for them to be altered.

We received a call saying that the original mother of our adult adopted son wanted to get in touch with him. He has never expressed any interest in his families of origin and we were afraid for him in case things didn't turn out well. We told the caller that he wasn't interested. We feel that we did what was best for him. Do you think we have any obligation to let him know?

162

Your son is an adult and has the right to make his own decisions. I cannot think of any other area of his life in which you would be able to make a decision on his behalf. I believe that it is only fair that he be given this information in order that he can exercise his freedom of choice and I think it is morally wrong of you to keep this from him. You also run the risk that he will find out eventually and be angry with you for taking this decision out of his hands.

When we adopted our daughter we were told that the original parents were intelligent and well educated. We expected that our adopted daughter, therefore, would be a high achiever. Instead she had no interest in education. When she was reunited with her original mother we learned that she was also unskilled and that we had been deceived by the adoption agency. Would we be able to sue them for misrepresentation?

I hope that you have not judged the 'value' of your child on the basis of her educational achievements or abilities. When you adopted her, it was, presumably, because you wanted to give a child a home. As parents, we have no way of knowing what the future holds for our children, but society expects parents to cherish their children, no matter what. Parental love is expected to be unconditional and does not have to be earned. Your adopted daughter is not responsible for your disappointment.

We adopted a child from another country and thought we were helping her by rescuing her from a life of disadvantage and poverty. But now that she is grown up and we see how it has affected her to be in a foreign culture and separated from her family and community, we feel that we were naïve and misguided. How can we make up for our mistake?

Many people agree with your sentiments and feel that exploitation has occurred in circumstances where children have been adopted into foreign countries. Being honest with your

163

daughter about your motives and your concern for her wellbeing, recognising her losses and doing everything you can to support her in acknowledging her identity will help her to heal the hurts which have occurred. You might also choose to use your experience to educate others.

As an adoptive parent I get tired of hearing so much talk about how important blood family is for children. Some people act as if the original mother is always the best person to raise a child and I know this isn't the case. We raised two adopted children and loved them more dearly than many parents who raise their own children. Why do people disregard the fact that it's possible to love children who are adopted just as much as one's own?

Because people emphasise the importance of blood family relationships, this doesn't mean that they are suggesting that relationships in adoptive families are less valuable, just that they are different. Of course, it's possible to love children to whom you are not related by blood. I don't believe that has ever been questioned. Some parents are competent and some are not, whether or not they are related to the child by blood. However, it is important to many adopted people to know who their blood relatives are.

When we adopted our daughter we thought that we were doing a good thing, but, now that I understand about the outcomes of adoption, I'm sorry that I was a part of a system which caused so much pain. I feel that I want to apologise to her original mother for taking her child from her. Do you think she'll forgive me?

I don't think you should blame yourself. I'm sure that you wanted what was best for your adopted daughter. I don't think it's about forgiving; I think it's more valuable to consider the adoption in its historical and social context and to focus on your motives and intentions. It's also useful to educate the community around the long term outcomes of adoption separation.

164

4b. Questions asked by family members

My husband is adopted and he recently heard from his original mother and father, who are now married. I didn't mind his having contact with them, but now it seems to be all he thinks about and all he talks about. I'm getting tired of it. I feel that I'm not important to him any more. Will I always have to take second place in his life?

When contact takes place between family members who have been separated by adoption, the initial emotions are often very intense and sometimes the behaviour takes on an almost obsessive appearance to those not directly involved. The feelings can be similar to those of an adolescent 'crush'. They can also resemble the feelings of grief following a death, when it seems that everything else in life is affected by the loss of the loved one. This preoccupation with the reunion, almost to the exclusion of other relationships, can last for some time, until a degree of trust is built up and the parties involved are able to reach an emotional plateau of sorts where their feelings level off. This is not to say that there won't be periods of strong emotion again from time to time, especially around particular events, like birthdays, but generally the initial intensity of the relationship does subside over time. During this period, those involved need all the support they can get from family and friends and so please try to be patient and generous. It is likely that his original parents are going to continue to play a part in his life and so it might be helpful to you to read about the impact of adoption on people's lives, so that you have a better idea of the emotional turmoil your partner may be experiencing.

My mother, who gave up her first child for adoption, died of cancer when she was in her forties. She had kept in touch with some of the other mothers she had known in the home for unmarried mothers and she told me that some of them also had developed cancer. Do you think there's a connection?

I have heard that mothers who have lost a child through adoption are more likely to develop cancer in later years than other women. As far as I know there is no research on this, but it is interesting to speculate as to whether this may have been related to their adoption separation experiences and buried grief.

My mother lost a child to adoption and she recently made contact with him. It was what she wanted and so I assumed she'd be happy when she found him. He seems to have welcomed the contact, but the whole thing has upset her so much that she's been crying a lot and drinking really heavily since the reunion. She was fine before all this happened. Making contact has caused nothing but trouble. Wouldn't it have been better if she had just left it in the past where it belonged?

It may be your perception that your mother was 'fine' before making contact with her son, but, in fact, the sadness that has come to the surface now has been buried since the separation from her child. When grief is buried, it causes stress and unhappiness, although this may not have been obvious to you over the years. It can also lead to physical illnesses and may be a factor in conditions such as chronic fatigue syndrome. Giving birth to a child is never in the past; it is an experience that mothers carry with them forever and so in one sense it is always in the present. Your mother is now expressing her grief and hopefully she'll move forward with her life in a positive way.

My sister got pregnant when she was a teenager and decided to give up her baby for adoption. I remember it very well. She seemed to me to have thought it all through and to be very sure that adoption was going to be the best option. She seemed quite calm about it all and believed she was acting sensibly. She never brought it up with me over the years and so I assumed that she was all right with it. Now, many years later, she's trying to tell me about her grief and suffering. She didn't look to me as if she was suffering. I'm baffled by all this talk of loss and grief. Can you help me to understand it?

While it may have appeared to you at the time that your sister was comfortable with her decision to allow her child to be adopted, for many women, the only way they could cope with what was happening, was to distance themselves from it emotionally. They presented a calm exterior because they thought that they had to go through with it and were trying to pretend that they were in control. For many of them, inside they were frightened and confused. After the birth, many original mothers buried their feelings yet again, sometimes because they didn't feel that they could face them, sometimes because they thought that they were doing what was expected of them, but mostly because they felt very alone with their experience and had no idea how they should be reacting. Imagine, if you can, not only keeping your feelings inside, but also burying your experience and not even talking about it. For many original mothers their hurt was eating away at them, but they were putting on a façade of being 'all right with it'. Then eventually they have the opportunity to get in touch with their feelings, to bring all that grief to the surface and to stop pretending. For many women it's like opening floodgates. All the feelings that they had suppressed over the years come to the surface, yet still those around them sometimes cannot empathise with their experience. That's why it's so important for mothers like your sister to talk with other people who have had the same experience. It would be useful for you to read about the impact of adoption on people's lives and the outcomes of suppressed grief. I hope that you can try to understand what the loss of her child has meant for your sister and to support her in her healing.

My mother has recently told us that she gave up a daughter for adoption when she was very young. I am totally shocked and

167

cannot understand how she could have lied to us for all those years. I feel that I can never trust her again and that she is not the person that I thought I knew and loved. I am so disappointed in her, that she taught us to be honest and yet all this time she was deceiving us. She wants to try to find her daughter but I've told her that I will never accept her as part of the family and so I don't even want to hear anything about it. This has totally wrecked our family. Can you understand that I just feel devastated by the whole thing?

Obviously it's been very difficult for you to come to terms with the fact that your mother has kept this from you. I can't answer for why she thought that was best, but I do know that mothers who have lost children to adoption often agonise over keeping it a secret. Usually it's such a painful subject for them that they can't bring themselves to try to explain to other people how it happened. For many women there is a lot of guilt and shame attached to their loss and it's just too hard to bring it out into the open. When they finally do pluck up the courage to be honest and to be known for who they really are, they take the risk that others will not understand and will judge them harshly. The loss of a child in a family has an impact on the whole family, as you have now realised. I hope that your family can work together to heal the pain and try to talk to your mother, so that you can understand what it has been like for her. It might also be helpful if you can read about the experiences of other mothers who lost children through adoption. Up until now your mother has not been able to find the words to tell you about your sister, but now she has decided to trust you enough to share this with you. I hope that you will understand that she needs your love and support. Please don't forget that she is still the same mother that you've always known, but now she has allowed you to know her more deeply. This is one more part of who your mother is, which she has been brave enough to share with you. She will be fragile for a while as it's a very emotional time, when a mother finally reveals the loss of her child. I hope that she will be able to find support when she needs it and that she won't have to go through yet another emotional trauma alone.

A year ago, my wife met the daughter she had given up for adoption before I met her. I was delighted for her to know her child again, but now my wife is telling me that she needs to be on her own. I fear that our marriage may be over. Why has this happened, when we have been happy together for twenty-five years? I'm trying to be understanding but it seems that having her daughter come back into her life has caused the break-up of my marriage.

It's quite common for a mother who is reunited with her child to begin to question other relationships in her life. It's difficult to explain in a few words why this so often happens. Many women were deeply affected both emotionally and psychologically by the experience of being separated from their children by adoption. Often, they then embarked on relationships without having addressed those issues of loss and grief. Many women buried their pain so deeply after being separated from their children that they felt as if they were leading a false life. The constant fear of discovery also has created a great deal of tension for them. When the reunion takes place they feel such a sense of relief and, for some, they finally have permission to be true to the person that they really are. Because their relationships with themselves change, it's inevitable that some of their relationships with other people in their lives will change also. Adopted adults often go through a similar experience after reunion occurs. I'm sure your wife did not try to deceive you in any way over the years and I'm sure that you have been happy together, but now it may be for her that she is finally able to explore who she really is and cast off the mask that she feels she has been wearing since she lost her child. For some women, this experience is life-altering and, because they feel like a different person, they are no longer able

169

to fulfil the role that they filled prior to the reunion. It may be that your wife needs some time to explore her emotions and to start to get in touch with her feelings again. I hope that you will be able to be patient and reassure her of your on-going love and support and that, in time, you and your wife will be able to resume your relationship, although it will not be exactly the same as it was before. It might be helpful if you are able to do some reading and learn more about the intensity of the emotions for women who are separated from their children by adoption and the impact on their sense of self that the reunion has.

My mother recently met the son she had given up for adoption. I'm happy for her that they have been reunited, but sometimes I know that the things he says and does hurt her. Do you think it's all right for me to talk to him about that?

I think it would be better if you talk to your mother about this issue. In the early stages of reunion, parents often find it difficult to set boundaries, as they are unsure of the relationship. It takes time for a level of comfort to be reached. Your mother may need some help to deal with her own grief. Perhaps you could suggest this to her and let her manage the relationship with her son in her own way.

Many years ago my son told me that his girlfriend was expecting his child. I offered to help in any way that I could. I begged him to stand by her and help her to raise my grandson but he refused and the baby was lost to adoption. I have never stopped thinking about my lost grandchild for all these years. Is there anything I can do to let my grandchild know that I care?

Sadly, it is seldom acknowledged that when an adoption takes place, grandparents lose a grandchild and they also can suffer from that loss. I hope that you will be able to talk to your son and encourage him to make every effort to contact his child. Perhaps if he understands that you have also suffered a loss, he

170

will think seriously about what he can do to ease your pain and to offer, not only his care and concern, but the care and concern of his family, to his grown-up child. Meanwhile, you can contact the adoption authorities in your area or the organisation that arranged the adoption and ask if you would be able to be given any information about your lost grandchild or if they would pass on a message from you. I'm sure your grandchild would be very moved to know that, even though you were not able to be involved at the time, you have carried him in your heart for so many years.

My wife is adopted and she suddenly decided for some reason that she wanted to try to find her original parents. It's upset her adoptive parents and caused nothing but trouble. I can't understand why she started all this. She had a good upbringing, shouldn't she have left the past in the past?

It's probably hard for you to understand, but for adopted people their adoption is never in the past; it's something that will always be a part of their lives and they live with it on a day-to-day basis. Your wife didn't 'start' anything when she decided to seek out her original parents. She is trying to reach a higher level of emotional well-being, find out about her original families and her heritage and piece together the events of her early life. For many adopted people it's very important that they try to do that and this is a time when she could benefit from the support of those around her. It can be a difficult and emotional time and I'm sure you'll want to be by her side as she deals with all of this. It might be helpful for you to try to learn about the impact of adoption separation on people's lives. Having had a 'good upbringing' does not mean that her original families are not important to her. It's possible for adopted people to acknowledge all of their various family connections.

My husband died recently. I knew that he had fathered a son before he met me and that the child had been adopted. His son made contact some years ago, but my husband refused to meet him, as he didn't want to upset our two daughters. Should I let his son know that he has died?

It's very sad that the reunion did not take place and I think you would be doing his son a favour by letting him know that his original father has died. You are in a position to give him some information about his father and explain his reasons for refusing the reunion. Although he will never know his original father, he may wish to make contact with his half-sisters and other family members.

My mother is eighty-two years old. She was contacted recently by the daughter she gave up for adoption when she was very young. My mother had never told us anything about this child. We have now met our lost sister and we are delighted to welcome her back into the family. My mother is absolutely thrilled to see her child again. My only sadness is that my mother may not have much time left to enjoy having her daughter in her life. Why is it that many adopted people leave it so late before they make contact with their original families?

That's a question that I have been asked often, but it's a difficult one to answer. Some adopted people are unaware of any buried feelings around their relationship with their original family members and don't see any advantage in contacting them. Some adopted people fear possibly having to confront unpleasant details about their beginnings in life. For some, it's about fear of the response they might receive from their original parents. Sometimes it's about fear of a negative reaction from their adoptive parents. Hopefully some of these fears can be dispelled with more community education. There is less secrecy and shame around adoption experiences these days and that helps to alleviate people's fears.

4c. Questions asked by professionals

I think it's wrong that parents who gave up children for adoption should have the right to know anything about their children, once those children become adults. They gave up the right to be parents. Why should they be allowed to interfere in their adult child's life?

I have never heard of a case where an original parent wanted to contact an adult adopted child for anything other than a generous and caring reason. Presenting someone with an invitation is not interfering. Those parents lost the right to raise their children to adulthood. Once those children become adults, however, then the matter of parental rights is no longer an issue. I believe that a reunion between adopted adults and their original parents allows all parties to confront their losses and experience the grieving process. This can release them from the constraints of repressed grief and allow them to move forward. Adults make their own choices in every area of their lives, but they can't make a free and informed choice if vital information is kept from them. It seems that there is a belief in the community that those parents should be condemned to some sort of lifelong punishment, for having done what they were told at the time was best for their children. If a married couple divorce, there is no law that prevents them from knowing about their children. Divorced parents are still parents even when they are no longer legally connected to each other and are actually expected to maintain a relationship with their children. When children are adopted, their original parents are still their parents, regardless of the fact that they are no longer legally connected to each other. In many cases a reunion would not have taken place if the child and the parent had not both been seeking out the other. Any legislation that supports those searches is, in my opinion, a matter of social justice and is undoubtedly in the best interests of all involved.

Don't you think that the effects of adoption have been overstated? Isn't adoption often used as an excuse for people who are just not coping with life in general?

Adoption may help to provide an explanation for people's behaviour. I firmly believe that adoption should never be used as an excuse and I agree that, unfortunately, this does sometimes happen. I'm unhappy about the degree to which those who have been separated from family members as a result of an adoption are portrayed (and sometimes portray themselves) as helpless victims. Adoption is often used as a justification for bitterness. Some people nurse a deep and abiding sense of resentment related to their adoption separation and they direct their energies into blaming others for perceived wrongs. I don't believe that these attitudes are helpful and, in fact, they often alienate the community in general, rather than educating and enlightening them. However, I think that for too long the impact of adoption was understated and misinterpreted and that now we have a deeper understanding of the degree of loss connected to adoption separation and the problems associated with not having grieved that loss. We still need to find ways to inform and educate our families, our communities, those in the helping professions and our politicians.

Surely it can't be all right for a mother who gave up a child for adoption to be able just to ring that person up once they become an adult?

A bank employee can call that person and offer them a credit card. If they don't want it, they can refuse that offer. Their original mother can call them and offer them information, affection, whatever she has to offer. If they don't want it, they can refuse that offer too. That's how adults manage their affairs. They make adult choices. While I appreciate that contact with one's original mother is a more serious matter than discussing credit cards, I find it difficult to understand why attempts are made to restrict contact between family members, when most of us accept and deal with contact from complete strangers throughout our adult lives. At least those who have been involved in adoptions have the choice to prepare themselves in advance for the possibility of contact and reunion with family members.

I know of a case where a mother contacted the adult daughter she had given up for adoption, only to find that her daughter didn't know that she was adopted. The telephone call from her original mother threw her into total chaos and has seriously disrupted her life and the lives of her adoptive parents. Surely in a case such as this, it would have been better to have checked with the adoptive parents first and avoided all this distress?

If distress has been caused to this young woman, let's look at who is responsible for that distress. The distress and disruption were caused by the original deceit, not by the introduction of the truth. Who is responsible for the deceit? The adoptive parents chose to lie to the child they had adopted and knew that they were taking the risk that someone would one day reveal the truth. They are the ones who have caused the disruption and distress, not the original mother. Sadly, it is becoming more and more common in our society for those who speak the truth to be blamed and for those who have lied to be defended. Frequently when there has been deceit and betrayal, which the guilty party has managed to conceal, the person who reveals the truth is castigated, while the liar is portrayed as the aggrieved party. This also happens frequently in adoption situations. Deceit and betrayal can be destructive to relationships, while confronting the truth can be therapeutic and constructive. In this case, the original mother has done her daughter a favour by offering her the opportunity to learn the truth and to deal with reality. I'm not surprised that the daughter is distressed and angry, but I hope that she is clear about where the responsibility for that lies.

Why encourage people to think of the past? Isn't it better for them to be helped to live in the present?

For those who have been separated from a family member because of an adoption, no matter how long ago it happened, their adoption experience is in the past, in the present and in the future. Anything that can help them to work through the issues which arise from having an adoption experience is worthwhile, in my opinion. Governments allowed adoptions to happen by enacting adoption legislation and I believe that they have a responsibility to assist those whose lives have been affected to manage the outcomes in a healthy, productive manner.

I've heard of so many bad reunion experiences. Isn't it sometimes better to let sleeping dogs lie rather than cause so much pain?

Apparently they used to tell the volunteers in the Territorial Army in Scotland that there's no such thing as bad weather, only the wrong clothes. In my opinion, there's no such thing as a bad adoption reunion experience, but I have heard of many cases of poor preparation. Some people find disappointment when they experience reunion, because they have allowed themselves to build up certain expectations and those are not met. Sometimes people misunderstand what has happened or can't see what has been gained from their experience. They sometimes think that the reunion has caused the pain, when in, fact, it was the original separation which caused the pain. There have been some people who have had some painful experiences following an adoption reunion, but painful experiences happen in everyone's life, sometimes as a result of adoption, sometimes not. Of course, there are risks in undertaking a reunion, but there are also valuable opportunities for growth.

Do you think it is ever a positive move to break off contact with the other party after a reunion has occurred?

First of all, I always believe that it is more advantageous for everyone that the reunion occurred than for it not to have occurred. I always advise people not to give up too easily, if there seem to be difficulties after reunion and to try to resolve them. Hopefully the two parties can work out a level and a method of contact on which they can both agree. In many situations, however, regardless of whether or not there has been an adoption, there are family members who choose not to keep in touch. Sometimes that has to be accepted. There are also cases where one party has threatened, assaulted or abused a family member. In situations like these, people have to take appropriate steps to protect themselves.

What about children who were abandoned with no record of who their parents are? Can they recover from that?

It's very sad that this has happened in some cases and I believe that personal recovery can still be achieved by acknowledging and working through the impact which their circumstances have had on their lives. Some choose to seek media exposure to try to locate their families and this is sometimes successful. The challenge for all of us is not only to confront and accept what life has given us, but to assess what we have made of our lives.

What about those who never meet?

I feel very sad for those who never meet. Some have not yet met because they have chosen not to seek. Others have not yet met because, while one party feels ready, the other does not. Some have searched unsuccessfully. A degree of personal satisfaction can be obtained, however, by doing all in one's power to effect a reunion or to connect in some way with the other person. Some people have to be satisfied with information and, in some situations, indirect contact made via an associate. For others the possibility of meeting has been denied them permanently because

177

of the death of the other party. Some have been able to build relationships with those who knew the deceased family member. For them at least there is a sense of finality, although it may not be the outcome for which they had hoped. The difficulty is in striking a balance between accepting the situation and not losing hope. It is best not to dwell to an unhealthy extent on what might have been and to be able to continue with a degree of inner peace in one's life.

I have heard that there is a higher rate of suicide, or suicide attempts, among those who have been separated by adoption, than in the general population. Is this true and, if so, can anything be done about it?

Anecdotal evidence suggests that this is the case. What I believe would be helpful is more education both in the general community and especially among professionals around the issues of loss and grief associated with adoption separation and the benefits of both personal and interpersonal recovery.

I'm a social worker and I worked for twenty-five years with homeless adolescents. I would estimate that at least half of them had been adopted. Do you have an explanation for this?

Many of those young people would have been adopted at a time when their issues of loss and grief were not acknowledged. We now understand that raising adopted children is not the same as raising children who are born into the family. Some have assumed that these difficulties were the result of genetics. However, the experiences of subsequent children born to parents who had lost children to adoption do not support this theory. Some have suggested that this happened as a result of poor parenting skills on the part of the adoptive parents. However, there have been many adopted children who have had stable family lives and have not become homeless as teenagers. We should explore and learn from these sad experiences.

178

I read that only a small percentage of the babies born to unmarried mothers in the 1960s and 1970s were adopted. Is that true?

While available research indicates that about 60% of babies born to unmarried mothers around that time were adopted, it's not possible to provide an accurate figure, because of the way information was collected. In most countries, common law or de facto relationships were not recognised and so any baby born to a mother who was not legally married would have been recorded as 'illegitimate'. Also, if a woman had been married and was separated and then later gave birth, although she would now be viewed as a 'single mother', her status would have been recorded at that time as 'married'. Some unmarried mothers were recorded as 'married', because they had told hospital staff that they were married, so that they would not be pressured to agree to adoption. Some mothers were married shortly after the birth of their 'illegitimate' child. In some cases, children of single mothers were 'adopted' informally within the family. Because of these anomalies, there is a lack of clarity around the percentage of babies born to single mothers who were legally adopted outside of the family. The level of social stigma attached to illegitimacy and its impact on the child's future was also a factor and this may have varied according to the social status of the mother's family.

How can people use their adoption experiences to make a positive contribution? How can they put their grief and their anger to work in a constructive way?

If adoption is talked about more openly, honestly and publicly, then the level of fear and ignorance in the community will decrease. Those who have experienced adoption separation can help themselves and others by talking about their experiences in an informed and respectful manner. In this way they can assist their own healing and play their part in educating the community.

~~~~~~~~~~~~~~~~

References

Berryman, Sarah, *Understanding Reunion: Reflections on Research from the Post-Adoption Resource Centre, NSW,* in Separation, Reunion, Reconciliation, Proceedings from the Sixth Australian Conference on Adoption, Brisbane, 1997

Condon, John, *Psychological disability in women who relinquish a baby for adoption,* Medical Journal of Australia, Vol.144, Feb 3, 1986.

Doka, Kenneth, *Disenfranchised Grief: Recognizing Hidden Sorrow,* Lexington Books, Lexington, MA., 1989

Inglis, K., *Living Mistakes – Mothers who consented to adoption,* Allen & Unwin, Sydney, 1984

Kauffman, Jeffrey, *Intrapsychic Dimensions of Disenfranchised Grief,* Chapter 3 in Disenfranchised Grief, edited by Kenneth Doka, Lexington Books, Lexington, MA., 1989

Kuhn, Dale, *A Pastoral Counselor Looks at Silence as a Factor in Disenfranchised Grief,* Chapter 21 in Disenfranchised Grief, edited by Kenneth Doka, Lexington Books, Lexington, MA., 1989

Lifton, Betty Jean, *Journey of the Adopted Self,* Basic Books, 1994.

Meagher, David, *The Counselor and the Disenfranchised Griever,* Chapter 27 in Disenfranchised Grief, edited by Kenneth Doka, Lexington Books, Lexington, MA., 1989

Nichols, Jane, *Perinatal Loss,* Chapter 11 in Disenfranchised Grief, edited by Kenneth Doka, Lexington Books, Lexington, MA, 1989.

Pavao, Dr Joyce Maguire, *Healing Stories,* in Adoption and Healing, Proceedings of the International Conference on Adoption and Healing, New Zealand Adoption Education and Healing Trust, 1997

Pine, Vanderlyn, *Death, Loss, and Disenfranchised Grief*, Chapter 2 in Disenfranchised Grief, edited by Kenneth Doka, Lexington Books, Lexington, MA., 1989

Raphael, Beverley, *The Anatomy of Bereavement*, Basic Books, New York, 1983

Shawyer, Joss, *Death by Adoption*, Cicada Press, New Zealand, 1979

Shawyer, Joss, *The Politics of Adoption*, Healthright, Vol.5, No.1, November 1985.

Silverman, Phyllis, *Helping Women Cope with Grief*, Sage Publications, California, 1981

Small, Joanne, *Working with Adoptive Families*, Public Welfare, Summer 1987

van Keppel, M., Midford, S. & Cicchini, M., *The Experience of Loss in Adoption*, Fifth National Conference, National Association for Loss and Grief, Perth, September, 1987.

Verrier, Nancy, *The Primal Wound: Legacy of Adoption*, presented at the American Congress International Convention, California, USA, April, 1991

Verrier, Nancy, *The Primal Wound*, Gateway Press, Baltimore, USA, 1993

Winkler, R. & van Keppel, M., *The Effect on the Mother of Relinquishing a Child for Adoption*, Third Australian Conference on Adoption, Adelaide, 1982.

Winkler, R., van Keppel, M., *Relinquishing Mothers in Adoption, Their long-term adjustment,* Melbourne Institute of Family Studies, Monograph no.3, 1984

Worden, J. W., *Grief Counselling and Grief Therapy*, Second Edition, Spring Publishing Co., New York,1991

About the author

Evelyn Robinson, MA, Grad Dip Ed, BSW, has both personal and professional experience of adoption separation and reunion. Evelyn gave birth to her son, Stephen, in Edinburgh, Scotland, in 1970 and he was adopted soon after his birth. Stephen and Evelyn were reunited in 1991 in Australia and continue to enjoy a close relationship. Evelyn has also been a professional social worker since 1996 and has been employed since that time as a counsellor and educator in the post-adoption field. She has always given generously of her time and energy to promote healing for those who have been separated by adoption and to educate the community around the long term outcomes of adoption separation. Evelyn has travelled within Australia and to New Zealand, the United Kingdom, Ireland, Canada and the United States, in her own time and at her own expense, providing training and information sessions to members of the adoption community, professionals, government departments and adoption support organisations. She has also presented conference papers on adoption-related topics in some of these locations and in Romania and South Korea. Her books inform the work of professionals around the world and are used as self-help manuals by those who have experienced adoption separation. While each person's response to an adoption separation is individual, some general exploration and understanding of the issues can be useful to everyone. Even when there has been no adoption, many adults suffer from separation losses and find themselves considering a meeting with someone with whom they have a genealogical connection. Evelyn's books are also for them. Through her international presentations and her books, Evelyn has made an enormous contribution to increasing awareness around the world of Australia's enlightened approach to adoption separation and reunion, now widely respected and admired. Evelyn was appointed in September, 2009 to the National Inter Country Adoption Advisory Group which meets with the Australian Attorney-General's Department, to advise on intercountry adoption policy and practice. Further information about Evelyn Robinson and her valuable work is available from www.clovapublications.com.